Essential Math Series

The Essential Guide to Competition Math
Counting and Probability

유하림(Harim Yoo) 지음

The Essential Guide to **Competition Math**
[Counting and Probability]

초판 발행 2022년 3월 25일

저자 유하림
발행처 헤르몬하우스
발행인 최영민

주소 경기도 파주시 신촌로 16
전화 031-8071-0088
팩스 031-942-8688
전자우편 hermonh@naver.com
출판등록 2015년 03월 27일
등록번호 제406-2015-31호
인쇄제작 미래피앤피

ISBN 979-11-91188-79-0   53410

Copyright © 2022 by Harim Yoo
First edition Printed 2022. Printed in Korea.

- 헤르몬하우스는 피앤피북의 임프린트입니다.
- 이 책의 어느 부분도 저작권자나 발행인의 승인 없이 무단 복제하여 이용할 수 없습니다.
- 파본 및 낙장은 구입하신 서점에서 교환하여 드립니다.
- 정가는 뒤표지에 있습니다.

Preface

To. 학부모님과 학생들께

The Essential Guide to Competition Math (Number Theory) 와 더불어, 이 교재는 해외 대학교를 준비하는 학생 중 수학(Mathematics)과 관련된 학과를 진학하려는 학생들에게 큰 도움을 주고자 작성하였습니다. 다양한 수학경시대회에서 출제되고 있는 문제들의 난이도는 흔히 얘기하는 킬러 문형들이 더 많은데, 입문용 교재에 들어가 있는 문제의 난이도는 초중급 난이도가 더 많아서, 이 둘 사이의 간격을 좁힐수 있는 방법이 무엇일까 고민하다가, Number Theory 교재와 마찬가지로, 준킬러 문형들을 많이 학습할 수 있는 교재가 필요하다는 결론을 내렸습니다.

이 교재는 현재 경시대회를 준비하려고 하는 학생들과 수업을 하면서, 계속해서 가다듬고 피드백 받고, 연구원을 통하여, 계속 문제 난이도 조절을 하다가, 이번 기회에 출간하게 되었습니다. 입문용 교재로 공부가 끝난 학생들에게 킬러 문형을 풀기 직전 연습을 해야 하는 문제들 위주로 작성을 했고, 여러 피드백을 받아보니, 준킬러 문형에 해당한 문제들이 훨씬 많이 포함하고 있어서, 상위권 학생들에게는 복습의 기회가 되고, 상위권으로 올라가야 할 학생들에게는 필요한 든든한 디딤돌 같은 역할을 하기에 적합하다는 평이 많았습니다.

특히, 경우의 수와 확률을 정확하게 구분하고, 이에 대한 수학적 도구를 잘 점검할 수 있도록 주제별로 구분하였고, 점화식(recurrence relation), 번사이드 보조정리(Burnside's lemma), 그리고 기댓값(expected value)의 응용까지 모두 다루다보니, 연구원 및 가르치는 학생들의 평은 "난이도가 꽤 있는 문제들뿐만 아니라, 생각을 필요로 하는 재밌는 문제들이 많다"였습니다.

이전 교재들과 마찬가지로 교재 제목인 Essential Guide가 암시하듯, 핵심 문제들로 구성되어있어, 150쪽 내외의 교재로 구성되었지만, 책을 구성하고 있는 문제들은 모두 하나하나 경시수학을 준비하려는 학생들에게 필요한 문제들입니다. 입문용 교재를 volume 1이라고 생각한다면, 이 교재는 volume 2, 그리고 추후 나올 교재들은 모두 volume 3, 4 등과 같은 방식으로 유기적으로 관계를 맺고 있는 교재들로 작업하고 있으니, 입문용 교재를 공부한 이후에, 이 교재로 학습하면 크게 도움이 되지 않을까 싶습니다.

이 교재를 출간할 수 있도록 '롤모델'로서 '강사'로서 성장할 수 있는 원동력을 주시는 심현성 대표님께 감사합니다. 또한, 이런 집필의 기회를 마련해주신 마스터프렙 권주근 대표님께 감사합니다. 또한, 현재 제 여러 교재 검수를 맡고 있는 든든한 안준규 제자에게도 감사의 마음을 전합니다. 언제나 든든한 지원군인 제 아내와 딸, 부모님께도 항상 감사합니다. 마지막으로, 제 삶에 이러한 기회를 주신 하나님께 감사드립니다. 앞으로도 더 좋은 교재를 만들어 견고하고 튼튼한 유하림 커리큘럼을 완성하겠습니다.

2022년 1월
유하림

이 책의 특징

유하림 커리큘럼 Essential Math Series 경시 시험 대비를 위한 책 중 AMC 10(12), CEMC, ARML Local, Purple Comet Math Meet, Spirit of Math and Stanford SMILE International Contest와 같은 시험을 대비하는 교재입니다. AMC 10을 이미 시작하는 8, 9, 10학년 한국 학생들이 AIME Qualification을 받기 위해 공부해야 하는 필독서가 되길 바라는 마음으로 집필하였습니다. 현재 미국 명문 Boarding School 및 국내외 외국인학교에 다니는 8, 9, 10학년 학생들이 AMC 10(12) 및 다른 경시 시험에서 실제로 적극적으로 사고(think)하고, 문제 풀이의 방향을 잡을 수 있길 바라면서 책을 썼습니다.

☝ 실력을 기르기에 최적화된 교재

경시 수학 관련하여 압구정 현장 강의에서 많은 학생들을 교육하였고, 실제로 이런 문제들을 포함한 수업을 듣다가, 경시 수학에 연을 맺어, MIT 및 Stanford와 같이 유수의 학교로 간 제자들이 많습니다. 위 제자들을 가르치며, 핵심 개념과 복잡한 문제풀이의 그 중간과정에서 가장 많이 고민했던 유형들의 문제들과 다양한 개념의 융합된 형태의 문제들을 적절히 섞어두었습니다. 특히, 준킬러 문형들이 많이 포함되어 있기 때문에, 해설지를 상세히 공부해가며, 여러 가지 측면으로 푸는 연습을 하길 바랍니다. 위 책은 현장 강의에서 가장 좋은 피드백을 받은 문제들 위주로 작성한 교재이므로, AMC 10/12의 Counting and Probability 문제들을 공략하기 위해 작성된 교재입니다.

✌️ 생각의 확장을 위한 교재

Counting and Probability를 배울 때, 쉽게 생각하는 부분부터 해서 현재 문제 출제 방향에 가장 적합하게 서술했으며, 실제 경시대회 문형들의 최고난이도 문제보다는 쉽게, 다만 그 문제를 풀기 위해 반드시 알아야 하는 방향을 제시하는 교재로 집필하였습니다. 문제 유형으로 나누어 설명하는 것보다, Counting and Probability의 주제들에 적용되는 다양한 사고방식을 서술하였으며, 이들이 어떻게 합쳐지면서 문제 풀이에 적용되는지 체감하며 공부할 수 있는 교재입니다.

🤟 유학 준비생을 위한 바로 그 교재

교과 수학보다 응용의 폭이 깊어서, 시작조차 엄두를 내지 못했던 유학생들과 그 준비생들에게 하나의 지름길이 될 수 있기를 희망하면서 집필한 책입니다. 노스웨스턴 대학교 학창시절 수학에 대한 열정을 뒤늦게 꽃피워 밤새워 공부했고, 저는 학생들을 더 잘 가르치고, 더 나은 미래로 이끌기 위해, AMC, AIME, Stanford SMILE, ARML, HMMT, PUMaC, SUMO와 같은 문제들을 동일한 열정으로 끊임없이 풀고 해석합니다. 여러분이 지금 보는 이 책은 제 현재 노력의 최선의 산실이며, 앞으로도 그러할 것입니다. 이 책을 통해 수학을 두려워하지 않고, 문제 해결을 즐거워하며, 이른 나이에 수학에 대한 열정을 꽃피우길 기대합니다.

CONTENTS

Preface   3
이 책의 특징   4

TOPIC 1 Basic Counting Tools   9
   1.1   One-to-one Correspondence 10
   1.2   Principle of Inclusion and Exclusion 11
   1.3   Addition or Multiplication 12
   1.4   Casework or Complements 14
   1.5   Circular Permutation 15
          Practice 16

TOPIC 2 Distinguishables and Indistinguishables   47
   2.1   Partition of Natural Numbers 48
   2.2   Partition of Sets 49
   2.3   Permutation allowing Repetition 50
   2.4   Combination allowing Repetition 51
          Practice 52

TOPIC 3 Extending to Probability 71

    3.1   Extending to Probability 72

    3.2   Conditional Probability 76

    3.3   Geometric Probability 77

           Practice 78

TOPIC 4 Special Themes 95

    4.1   Recurrence Relation 96

    4.2   Burnside's Lemma 97

    4.3   Expected Value and Random Walk 99

           Practice 100

TOPIC 5 Mixed Practice 121

           Practice 122

작가의 Recommendation

이 글을 쓰며, 노스웨스턴대학교 학부 시절을 돌이켜보니, 밤을 지새워 가며 수학 공부를 할 때, 문제가 풀렸을 때의 그 희열감이 참 대단했다는 생각이 듭니다. 그 희열감을 다시 느껴보고자, 문제를 풀다가 막히고, 또 한 걸음 나아갔다가 막히는 등, 이런 과정을 여러 시간 동안 고민하다 보니, 가끔은 참으로 비효율적이라는 생각이 들곤 했습니다.

'내가 어린 시절, 문제 풀이에 집중하는 경시 문제들을 푼다면, 대학교 입학뿐 아니라, 대학 생활에서 수학 수업과 관련된 생활이 수월했을까?'

학부 시절 만나는 대다수의 수학과 관련 문제들은 증명 문제 스타일이거나 해석학과 관련한 문제들이었지만, 조합론과 그래프 이론 등 경시대회에서 나오는 주제와 겹쳐지는 시험에 등장한 문제들은 요즘의 경시대회에서 만나볼 수 있는 문제들의 스타일과 비슷하다는 느낌이 들었던 기억이 많이 납니다. 다른 말로 해보자면, 경시수학을 공부함으로써 대학 입학뿐 아니라, 대학교에서 이수하는 수학 관련 수업에도 도움이 많이 되겠다는 생각입니다. 뿐만 아니라, 대학교에 가서도 큰 도움이 된다는 점은 제가 가르친 학생들에게서도 충분히 엿볼 수 있었습니다. 이러한 점 때문에 저는 경시수학을 가르치는 것에 매력을 느꼈고, 이런 교재들을 작성할 수 있게 되었습니다.

근본적으로 수학 문제를 풀다 보면, 문제해결 능력이 무엇인가 생각을 해보게 됩니다. '내가 가지고 있는 도구(Tool)는 무엇이고, 이러한 도구를 어떻게 사용해야 할까?'라는 생각이 들곤 합니다. 끙끙대며 푸는 시간이 오래 걸릴수록, 문제 출제자의 의도가 무엇일까 생각하게 되고, 내가 제대로 된 방향으로 문제를 풀고 있는지 의심이 들지만, 문제를 풀고 난 후에는 내가 알고 있는 생각의 재료를 잘 활용하여 결국은 풀린다는 확신이 들게 됩니다.

독자 여러분이 반드시 알아야 할 점은 경시대회에서 좋은 성적을 거둬야만 좋은 대학교에 입학하게 되는 것이 아니라는 점입니다. 다만, 경시수학을 공부한 학생들에게 주어지는 이득은 꽤 큽니다. 더 좋은 학교를 지원할 수 있는 기회를 얻기도 하고, 여름 방학동안 전 세계의 다양한 친구들과 함께 Math Camp를 다녀올 수도 있습니다.

"경시수학은 수학 천재들만 공부하는 것이 아닌가요?"라는 질문에는 감히 답변을 드리자면, 충분히 생각을 즐기고, 위에 서술한 것과 같이, '생각의 재료'를 가지고 '문제해결'에 적용하는 것을 즐기는 학생이라면, 누구나 해볼만한 '즐거운 도전'입니다. 특히, 이 교재를 선택한 독자 여러분들은 경시대회에 나오는 다양한 수학 문제들을 즐기고, 이 과정에서 '문제 해결 능력'이라는 것을 길러보는 기회로 삼기 바랍니다.

끝으로, Arthur Engel 교수님이 집필한 〈Problem Solving Strategies〉의 Chapter 1 도입부에 다음과 같이 적혀 있는 글을 소개합니다.

"In fact, problem solving can be learned only by solving problems. But it must be supported by strategies by the trainer."

이 글을 읽는 독자 여러분, 즐겁게 수학 공부하시기 바랍니다!

TOPIC 1

Basic Counting Tools

1.1 One-to-one Correspondence

One-to-one correspondence is one of the basic tools we use when we deal with discrete mathematics. (Here, discrete mathematicis means the branch of mathematics dealing with something that is "countable.")

What we try to do here is to connect $\{1, 2, 3, 4, 5, \cdots\}$ to $\{a, b, c, d, \cdots\}$, where 1 corresponds to a, 2 to b, and so on. The general rule to follow is that adding, subtracting, multiplying, or dividing by a constant does NOT change the number of items in the list. Have a look at the following example.

Example Find the number in the list of $1, 4, 7, 10, 13, \cdots, 100$.

Step-by-Step Solution

#1. Notice that each consecutive number has the difference of 3.
#2. Add 2 to each number to get $3, 6, 9, 12, 15, \cdots, 102$.
#3. Divide the new list by 3 to get $1, 2, 3, 4, \cdots, 34$.
#4. There are 34 numbers in the final list, so there must be 34 numbers in the original list.

Example Find the number in the list of $\frac{1}{3}, 1, \frac{5}{3}, \cdots, 67$.

Step-by-Step Solution

#1. Notice that each consecutive number has the numerator has the difference of 2 when we make a denominator of 3.
#2. Multiply 3 to the list to get $1, 3, 5, \cdots, 201$.
#3. Notice that each consecutive pair has the difference of 2.
#4. Add 1 or subtract 1. In this book, we would add 1. (You can also get the same answer when you subtract 1 from this list.)
#5. The new list is $2, 4, 6, \cdots, 202$.
#6. Divide it by 2 to get $1, 2, 3, \cdots, 101$.
#7. Conclude that there are 101 numbers in the final list. Therefore, there are 101 numbers in the original list.

Example If a and b are elements of $\{0, 1, 2\}$, show that $a - b + c = 0$ and $a + b' + c = 2$ have the same number of solution triples, where $b' = 2 - b$.

Step-by-Step Solution

#1. Notice that $b' = 2 - b$ has one-to-one correspondence between b and b'.
#2. $(a, b', c) = (2, 0, 0), (0, 2, 0), (0, 0, 2), (1, 1, 0), (1, 0, 1), (0, 1, 1)$. There are six solutions to (a, b', c).
#3. Conclude that there are 6 triples (a, b, c) as well, due to one-to-one correspondence.

1.2 Principle of Inclusion and Exclusion

Principle of inclusion and exclusion is used most of the times when there might be "overlaps." If there are two sets A and B, then $n(A \cup B) = n(A) + n(B) - n(A \cap B)$ where $A \cup B$ is the union of A and B, and $A \cap B$ is the intersection of A and B.

Example Let $A = \{1, 2, 3, 4\}$ and $B = \{3, 4, 5, 6\}$. Find the size of $A \cup B$, i.e., $n(A \cup B)$.

Step-by-step Solution
#1. First, $n(A \cup B) = n(A) + n(B) - n(A \cap B)$.
#2. Notice that $A \cap B = \{3, 4\}$, so $n(A \cap B) = 2$.
#3. Therefore, $n(A \cup B) = 4 + 4 - 2 = 6$ where $A \cup B = \{1, 2, 3, 4, 5, 6\}$.

Example Let $A = \{1, 2, 3\}$, $B = \{2, 3, 4\}$, $C = \{3, 4, 5\}$. Find the size of $A \cup B \cup C$, i.e., $n(A \cup B \cup C)$.

Step-by-step Solution
#1. $n(A \cup B \cup C) = n(A) + n(B) + n(C) - n(A \cap B) - n(B \cap C) - n(C \cap A) + n(A \cap B \cap C)$, by the Principle of Inclusion and Exclusion.
#2. $n(A \cup B \cup C) = 3 + 3 + 3 - 2 - 2 - 1 + 1 = 5$ where $A \cup B \cup C = \{1, 2, 3, 4, 5\}$.

Another application of P.I.E is "De Morgan's Law," which is useful when we take the intersection of two or more complements.

$$A^c \cap B^c = (A \cup B)^c \text{ or } A^c \cup B^c = (A \cap B)^c$$

Example If $U = \{1, 2, 3, 4, 5\}$, $A = \{1, 2, 3\}$, and $B = \{3, 4, 5\}$, find $n(A^c \cap B^c)$ where A^c is the set of elements that does not contain any element of A, and B^c is the set of elements that does not contain any element of B.

Step-by-step solution
#1. Use De Morgan's Law to compute $n(A^c \cap B^c)$.
#2.

$$\begin{aligned} n(A \cup B)^c &= n(U) - n(A \cup B) \\ &= n(U) - (n(A) + n(B) - n(A \cap B)) \\ &= 5 - (3 + 3 - 1) \\ &= 0 \end{aligned}$$

#3. It is easy to check that $A^c = \{4, 5\}$ and $B^c = \{1, 2\}$, so that there is no element in their intersection.

1.3 Addition or Multiplication

The fundamental tools in counting are addition and multiplication. In other words, subtraction and division are tools to get rid of overcounts. So, when do we add? When do we multiply? The following rules, not mathematically rigorous, can help us decide when to add or multiply.

- $+$: when we have to "casework," or when arithmetic "structure" is not repeated.

- $\times$: when counts are "ongoing," or when arithmetic "structure" is repeated.

Example If there are two possible ways to reach from A to B, and three possible ways to reach from B to C. In how many ways can we reach from A to C, assuming the path already used will not be chosen again?

Step-by-step Solution
#1. There are two paths to choose from A to B. Now, ask yourself a question whether the counts are completed.
#2. We answer the above question as "no," so we keep multiplying by 3, the number of paths from B to C.
#3. Hence, there are $2 \times 3 = 6$ ways to readch from A to C.

Example If there are two menus for lunch, and three menus for dinner, in how many ways can a glutton eat for lunch and dinner, assuming that he or she eats at least one menu for lunch and dinner, respectively?

Step-by-step Solution
#1. For lunch, there are $\binom{2}{1} + \binom{2}{2} = 3$ different ways for the glutton to choose for lunch. This is a typical illustration of casework. In the first case of when he or she chooses only one menu, then there are $\binom{2}{1}$ ways for him or her. On the other hand, in the second case of when he or she choose two menus, then there is $\binom{2}{2}$ way to choose. Since these two cases are disjoint, we add these two.
#2. For dinner, there are $\binom{3}{1} + \binom{3}{2} + \binom{3}{3} = 7$ different ways for the glutton to choose for dinner with the similar caseworks shown in the previous step.
#3. At #1, ask yourself whether the counts are done. You should answer it no, since the glutton did not choose anything for his or her dinner.
#4. This is the direct signal to multiply, so we have $3 \times 7 = 21$ number of ways for the glutton to eat lunch and dinner satisfying the given condition.

The crucial idea about learning how to count, especially knowing when to add or multiply, can be taught by practices. However, there are some helpful advice to follow.

- It's always best to write down specific cases, even though we are counting in abstract notion. For instance, in the earlier example, if you choose a specific path from A to B, then draw this in a diagram and see what happens next.

- If your gut feeling tells you 'Then, what?', it is highly likely that your count is not completed. As anyone can feel this from experience, if you hear your inner voice "then,", it must be multiplication.

Example Given a square region cut off by four congruent smaller squares, if each of the four regions are colored with either yellow, brown and blue, in how many configurations will any of the adjacent regions sharing an edge not have the same color? (Not all three colors should be used.)

Step-by-step Solution

#1. Let any of the smaller square be colored with three possibilities. Let's say it's brown.
#2. Any of the adjacent square can be colored with two possibilities. Let's say it's yellow.
#3. The third square, not adjacent to the square colored first, can be colored either brown or blue. This is the moment when arithmetic structure changes. Have a look at explanations illustrated next in detail.
#4. If it is colored brown, then the fourth square can be colored as yellow and blue. If it is colored blue, then the fourth square can be colored as yellow.
#5. Hence, there are $3 \times 2 \times (1 + 1 \times 1) = 18$ ways in total.

Number of cases	3	2	1 / 1	2 / 1
Specific case	Brown	Yellow	Brown / Blue	Yellow, Blue / Yellow

1.4 Casework or Complements

Other than the basic tools of + and ×, there are two special techniques we employ when performing case enumeration or complementary counting. Let's have a look at the first technique. Caseworks are

- exhaustive; skipping no case untouched;

- comprehensive; reaching to the case where the given condition laid out in a problem is not met.

Example If a and b are integers, compute the number of distinct pairs (a, b) such that $ab - a - b = 7$.

Step-by-step Solution
#1. By adding 1 to the both sides of the equation, we get $ab - a - b + 1 = 8$, which turns into $(a-1)(b-1) = 8$.
#2. Now, we perform caseworks on the signs of $a - 1$ and $b - 1$. They can both be positive or negative.
#3. If they are both positive, then $(a-1, b-1) = (1, 8), (2, 4), (4, 2)$, and $(8, 1)$.
#4. If they are both negative, then $(a-1, b-1) = (-1, -8), (-2, -4), (-4, -2)$, and $(-8, -1)$.
#5. Hence, there are 8 total distinct pairs of (a, b) satisfying the given condition.

On the other hand, the other tool is known as "complementary counting." We take everything in, and get rid of the counts that are not part of the condition. This complementary counting can go through slight correction so as to be utilized in other counting problems as well.

Example Compute the number of three-digit whole numbers that uses 1 as its digit at least once.

Step-by-step Solution
#1. There are 900 three-digit whole numbers in total.
#2. There are $8 \times 9 \times 9 = 648$ three-digit whole numbers, never using 1 as its digit(s).
#3. Hence, there are 252 three-digit whole numbers that uses 1 as its digit as least once.
#4. Or, we casework. If a number uses 1 once, then we may get 1☐☐, ☐1☐, and ☐☐1. Hence, there are $81 + 72 + 72 = 225$ whole numbers that use 1 only once.
#5. If a number uses 1 twice, then we may get 11☐, 1☐1, ☐11. Hence, there are $9 + 9 + 8 = 26$ whole numbers that use 1 twice.
#6. If a number uses 1 three times, then we get 111. Hence, in total, there are $225 + 26 + 1 = 252$ whole numbers satisfying the given condition.

1.5 Circular Permutation

When we arrange n number of objects in a row, we count using "permutation" or regular "factorial" notation, basically counting objects in rectilinear arrangement, i.e,

$\underbrace{\square\square\cdots\square}_{n \text{ objects in a row}}$.

Circular permutation, on the other hand, considers some of the arrangements as overcounts. Hence, we count this employing two different techniques, coined terms of which are not out of formal mathematics education but still provide some insights for students to understand.

- "*Conveyor belt*" method : in order to understand this method, think about a conveyor belt or sushi place with round table. Imagine we start with a sequence of four objects $(1, 2, 3, 4)$. Then, as the conveyor belt moves, it turns into $(2, 3, 4, 1)$, $(3, 4, 1, 2)$, and $(4, 1, 2, 3)$, all of which are "equivalent" in essence. Hence, we group all these into a single bundle to call it "$(1, 2, 3, 4)$." In other words, we arrange four objects as if there is no restriction whatsoever. Then, we delete overcounts by dividing the original count by 4, which is the size of the conveyor belt. Hence, $\frac{4!}{4} = 3!$ is the number of arrangements of four objects around the circular table.

- "*Observer*" method : let's continue with the same assumption with four objects. We choose our favorite object to be our "observer." Let 1 be our observer. Then, as soon as this 1 is placed, now all three seats will be considered as rectilinear configuration from 1's perspective. Hence, we simply take into account the number of different configurations counted by 1's perspective, which happens to be $3!$.

Example Compute the number of distinct arrangements of 5 people, including Bob and Bo, around a circular table such that Bob and Bo must be adjacent to one another.

Step-by-step Solution
#1. Think about a conveyor belt with five people. We have (Bob, Bo, $\square$, $\square$, $\square$), (Bo, $\square$, $\square$, $\square$, Bob), ($\square$, $\square$, $\square$, Bob, Bo), ($\square$, $\square$, Bob, Bo, $\square$), and ($\square$, Bob, Bo, $\square$, $\square$).
#2. There are $\frac{3! \times 5}{5}$, in the previous step. However, Bob and Bo can switch their seats, i.e., (Bo, Bob, $\square$, $\square$, $\square$), (Bob, $\square$, $\square$, $\square$, Bo), ($\square$, $\square$, $\square$, Bo, Bob), ($\square$, $\square$, Bo, Bob, $\square$), and ($\square$, Bo, Bob, $\square$, $\square$). Since arithmetic structure is exactly equivalent, we multiply by 2 to get $2 \times 3! = 12$ number of arrangements satisfying the given condition.
#3. Or, let Bob be seated as an observer. Then, Bo can sit in two seats. As soon as he is seated, there are three seats available for three people, so there are $2 \times 3! = 12$ ways for all five people to be seated around a circular table such that Bob and Bo are adjacent to each other.

Practice

1. Find the number of 4-tuples of integers (a, b, c, d) satisfying

$$a + b + c + d = 6$$

where $a \geq 1$, $b \geq 1$, $c \geq 1$ and $d \geq 1$.

(A) 5   (B) 10   (C) 15   (D) 20   (E) 25

2. For $0 \leq a, b, c \leq 9$, compute the number of 3-tuples of (a, b, c) satisfying

$$a - b + c = -7$$

(Hint: Use 1-to-1 correspondence and let $b' = 9 - b$.)

(A) 2   (B) 4   (C) 6   (D) 8   (E) 10

3. Let $A = \{0, 1, 4, 9, \cdots, 2025\}$ be an ordered set containing finite number of perfect squares. Compute $||A||$, where $||X||$ refers to the number of elements in a set X.

(A) 44 \qquad (B) 45 \qquad (C) 46 \qquad (D) 47 \qquad (E) 48

4. 2022 is an even integer with even number of digits, since the last digit is even and there are 4 digits in total. Compute the sum of the digits of 100th positive even integer with an even number of digits.

(A) 4 \qquad (B) 6 \qquad (C) 8 \qquad (D) 10 \qquad (E) 12

5. 999 is an odd integer with odd number of digits, since it ends with 9 and there are 3 digits in total. Compute the sum of the digits of 100th positive odd integer with an odd number of digits.

(A) 19   (B) 20   (C) 21   (D) 22   (E) 23

6. Given a sequence $\{x_i\} = \{2, 1, 2, 1, 2, 2, 2, 1, 2, 2, 2, 2, 2, 2, \cdots\}$ of the size 50 integers, where $1 \leq i \leq 50$ for $i \in \mathbb{N}$, defined by

$$\begin{cases} x_i = 1 \text{ if i is a power of 2.} \\ x_i = 2 \text{ if otherwise.} \end{cases}$$

compute the sum of all elements in the finite sequence.

(A) 91   (B) 92   (C) 93   (D) 94   (E) 95

7. The positive four-digit integers, which use each of the four digits 0, 1, 2, and 3 exactly once, are ordered from least to greatest. Compute the difference between the 7th term and 13th term.

(A) 111   (B) 333   (C) 555   (D) 777   (E) 999

8. The nth triangular number, known as T_n, is an integer obtained by adding all positive integers less than or equal to a given positive integer n, i.e., $T_n = \sum_{k=1}^{n} k$. Assume that a sequence
$$\{x_i\} = \{-1, 1, -1, 1, 1, -1, 1, 1, 1, -1, 1, 1, 1, 1, -1, \cdots\}$$
is defined by
$$\begin{cases} x_i = -1 \text{ if } i = T_p \text{ for } p \geq 1, p \in \mathbb{N} \\ x_i = 1 \text{ if otherwise.} \end{cases}$$
Then, the sum of all sequential terms of the first 2021 terms is $\overline{abcd}$. Compute $a + b + c + d$.

(A) 14   (B) 17   (C) 20   (D) 23   (E) 26

9. Out of all positive triangular numbers smaller than or equal to 2022, how many numbers are even?

(A) 30 (B) 31 (C) 32 (D) 33 (E) 34

10. Given a sequence $\{k^2, (k+1)^2, (k+2)^2, \cdots, 1936\}$, which can only be written as either strictly increasing or strictly decreasing order, if there are 17 distinct perfect squares, compute the sum of all possible values of k.

(A) -30 (B) -31 (C) -32 (D) -33 (E) -34

11. If five people select one distinct subject out of five different ones - History, Math, Physics, Biology, and Linguistics, in how many ways will the first person not choose History <u>and</u> the last person not choose Math?

(A) 72 (B) 75 (C) 78 (D) 81 (E) 84

12. If five people must select one subject out of five different ones - History, Math, Physics, Biology, and Linguistics, in how many ways will the first person not choose History <u>or</u> the last person not choose Math?

(A) 102 (B) 105 (C) 108 (D) 111 (E) 114

13. At a school with 100 mathletes, 50 are taking Geometry, 70 are taking Combinatorics, and 80 are taking Number Theory. No mathlete is taking all three subjects at the same time. Compute the number of mathletes who are studying both Combinatorics and Geometry.

(A) 0 (B) 10 (C) 20 (D) 30 (E) 40

14. There are 150 people at the gym. 110 are using flat bench, 70 are using the power rack, and 95 are using barbells. Everyone is using at least one of these three. Some people are using only *two* at a time for supersets. 30 are using both bench and rack. 25 are using both rack and barbells. 40 are using both barbells and flat bench. How many people are using all three?

(A) 5 (B) 10 (C) 15 (D) 25 (E) 30

15. In a kindergarden with 100 kids, 60 like swimming, 70 like playing soccer, 80 like painting, and 90 like playing in a playground. No kid likes all four. How many kids in the kindergarden like swimming and painting?

(A) 0   (B) 10   (C) 20   (D) 30   (E) 40

16. There are 30 students in a playgroup. There are 3 kids who have not watched "Octonauts" nor "Peppa Pig" at all. If there are twice as many kids having watched Peppa Pig as kids having watched Octonauts, and 3 kids have watched both programs, how many kids only watched Peppa Pig?

(A) 14   (B) 17   (C) 20   (D) 23   (E) 26

17. Compute the number of distinct terms in the expansion of

$$(x_1 + x_2 + x_3 + x_4)(y_1 + y_2 + y_3)(z_1 + z_2 + z_3 + z_4)$$

(A) 11 (B) 22 (C) 24 (D) 48 (E) 56

18. Find the number of distinct terms in the expansion of

$$(x_1 + x_2 + x_3 + x_4)(y_1 + y_2 + y_3)(z_1 + z_2 + z_3 + z_4)$$

such that the sum of indices is <u>even</u>. For instance, $x_1 y_1 z_1$ has the sum of 3 for their indices.

(A) 11 (B) 22 (C) 24 (D) 48 (E) 56

19. Compute the number of distinct triples of positive integers (x, y, z) satisfying $3x + 2y + z = 20$.

(A) 20 \qquad (B) 22 \qquad (C) 24 \qquad (D) 26 \qquad (E) 28

20. In how many ways can five people - grandfather, grandmother and three grandchildren - be seated in two rows of three chairs each, such that there must be one adult in each row?

(A) 72 \qquad (B) 144 \qquad (C) 196 \qquad (D) 225 \qquad (E) 432

21. Compute the number of distinct triples of positive integers (x, y, z) satisfying $3x + 2y + z = 20$ and $x \leq y \leq z$.

(A) 9   (B) 10   (C) 11   (D) 12   (E) 13

22. Bob and Bo should choose a new pair of socks and shoes, three kinds each with different stripes and shapes except there are only two colors to choose, either black or white, and they want pairs of socks and shoes in different stripes and shapes, while the colors should not be uniform for any kid. For example, a pair of red socks and red shoes are not allowed. In how many ways can they choose to wear pairs of socks and shoes?

(A) 72   (B) 144   (C) 196   (D) 225   (E) 256

23. If there are roman numerals I, II, III, and IV "fixed" in the first row and arabic numerals 1, 2, 3, 4 in the second row, compute the number of arrangements of roman numerals and arabic numerals such that inputs in every column are never matched, as shown in the figure below. (Arabic numerals are not fixed, yet roman numerals are.)

I	II	III	IV
2	4	1	3

(A) 7 (B) 8 (C) 9 (D) 10 (E) 11

24. The given hexagon tessellations are filled with infinitely many hexagons, also known as "honeycomb." Let there be a vertex P. Define a "move" as a directed walk along the edge from one vertex to its adjacent vertex. If the edge used in any "move" cannot be selected again, compute the total number of paths that can be traced after six "moves" that start from P, except the paths that return to the initial point. (Assume that similar paths with different directions are all distinguished.)

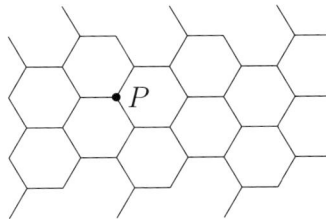

(A) 90 (B) 96 (C) 102 (D) 108 (E) 114

25. How many ways are there to divide a group of four athletes among the basketball team, the soccer team, and the volleyball team? Basketball and soccer team may have any number from 0 to 4 athletes on them, but volleyball team must have at least one athlete.

(A) 40 (B) 56 (C) 60 (D) 65 (E) 84

26. In a set of the first ten integers $\{1, 2, 3, 4, 5, 6, 7, 8, 9, 10\}$, in how many triples (x, y, z) can be chosen from the set such that $x \leq y < z$? (As suggested in the inequality, a number can be repeated.)

(A) 121 (B) 144 (C) 165 (D) 196 (E) 225

27. In a set of five integers $\{1, 2, 3, 4, 5\}$, in how many triples (x, y, z) can be chosen from the set such that $x \leq y \leq z$? (As suggested in the inequality, a number can be repeated.)

(A) 30   (B) 35   (C) 40   (D) 45   (E) 50

28. Given six digits $\{1, 2, 3, 3, 4, 5\}$, how many different six-digit numbers are there such that it is divisible by 4, only using the given digits? (For example, 145332 is divisible by 4.)

(A) 40   (B) 50   (C) 60   (D) 70   (E) 80

29. Five identical-looking circular coins are already arranged in a plane so that no two of them overlap nor touch, and no three of them have a tangent line in common. What is the total number of lines that are tangent to at least two of the given coins?

(A) 40 (B) 50 (C) 60 (D) 70 (E) 80

30. Find the number of distinct non-degenerate triangles with integer side lengths such that the perimeter is 12.

(A) 1 (B) 2 (C) 3 (D) 4 (E) 5

31. How many three-digit whole numbers satisfy the property that the middle digit is the average of the first and the last digits?

(A) 30 (B) 35 (C) 40 (D) 45 (E) 50

32. Bob plans to arrange three cards, labeled as A, B, and C, and six cards, labeled with numbers 1 through 6, such that there are exactly two number-cards between consecutive pair of alphabet-cards, as shown in the following figure. If there are n number of arrangements of nine cards that Bob's plan be satisfied, compute $n/10$.

$$\boxed{1}\boxed{A}\boxed{2}\boxed{3}\boxed{B}\boxed{4}\boxed{5}\boxed{C}\boxed{6}$$

(A) 1024 (B) 1296 (C) 1440 (D) 1960 (E) 2250

33. Six people, including Bob and Bo, are arranged around a circular table. Compute the number of ways of different arrangements of these people such that there must be two people between Bob and Bo.

(A) 24 (B) 36 (C) 48 (D) 60 (E) 72

34. Twelve people, including Bob and Bo, are arranged in a square table, where three people sit in each side. If the number of ways of different arrangements of these people's seats if Bob and Bo must be seated in opposite seats is written in n-digit number, find n.

(A) 8 (B) 9 (C) 10 (D) 11 (E) 12

35. Bob is organizing a race around a circular track and wants to put 3 water stations at 9 possible spots around the track. He doesn't want any 2 water stations to be next to each other because that would be inefficient. How many ways are possible?

(A) 30 (B) 35 (C) 40 (D) 45 (E) 50

36. How many different right triangles whose sides are parallel to the x-axis or y-axis can be formed by connecting four of the lattice points shown in the following set of dots?

(A) 100 (B) 144 (C) 196 (D) 256 (E) 324

37. In how many ways can three people - Ann, Ben, and Dan - be seated in a row of eight chairs if any pair of the three refuses to sit in consecutive seats?

(A) 96   (B) 100   (C) 104   (D) 108   (E) 120

38. Find the number of functions from the set $\{1, 2, 3, 4\}$ to itself such that $f(f(x)) = x$ for all $1 \leq x \leq 4$.

(A) 8   (B) 9   (C) 10   (D) 11   (E) 12

39. There are two male adults, two female adults, and one cat seated around a round table. If a cat must be surrounded by people with different gender, compute the total number of valid arrangements. Two arrangements are distinguishable if one cannot rotate one arrangement so that it looks like equal to the other arrangement.

(A) 2   (B) 4   (C) 8   (D) 12   (E) 16

40. How many ways are there to arrange five black marbles and three white marbles around a round table? Two arrangements are distinguishable if one cannot rotate one arrangement so that it looks like equal to the other arrangement.

(A) 7   (B) 8   (C) 9   (D) 10   (E) 11

Solution

1. (B)

Let $a = a' + 1$, $b = b' + 1$, $c = c' + 1$, and $d = d' + 1$. Then, $a' + b' + c' + d' = 2$ is one-to-one corresponding to $a + b + c + d = 6$. Hence,

$$a' + b' + c' + d' = 2$$
$$2 + 0 + 0 + 0 = 2$$
$$1 + 1 + 0 + 0 = 2$$

Now, $(2, 0, 0, 0)$ can be rearranged in four different fashions. Likewise, $(1, 1, 0, 0)$ can be rearranged by six different fashions. Hence, there are ten different tuples for (a', b', c', d'), so we conclude there are ten tuples for (a, b, c, d) as well.

2. (C)

Following the hint, we first notice that $b' = 9 - b$ makes one-to-one correspondence between b and b'. Now, $a + b' - 9 + c = -7$ turns into $a + b' + c = 2$. Also, if $0 \leq b \leq 9$, then $0 \leq b' \leq 9$, by translation property. Hence,

$$a + b' + c = 2$$
$$2 + 0 + 0 = 2$$
$$1 + 1 + 0 = 2$$

First, $(2, 0, 0)$ can be rearranged into three different tuples. Second, $(1, 1, 0)$ can be rearranged into three different tuples. Hence, there are six different tuples for (a, b', c), which has one-to-one correspondence with (a, b, c). Therefore, there are six tuples for (a, b, c).

3. (C)

Other than adding or subtracting, we can deduce that taking a square root is also one-to-one. In fact, if $y = \sqrt{x}$, this is a strictly-increasing function for $x \geq 0$, so it must be one-to-one. In particular,

$$\{0, 1, 4, 9, \cdots, 2025\} = \{\sqrt{0}, \sqrt{1}, \sqrt{4}, \cdots, \sqrt{2025}\}$$
$$= \{0, 1, 2, \cdots, 45\}$$
$$= \{x_1, x_2, x_3, \cdots, x_{46}\}$$

where x_i is the ith element in the set $\{0, 1, 2, \cdots, 45\}$. There are 46 integers in a set.

4. (D)

First, from 10 to 98, there are 45 even numbers in total. In order to count that there are 45 even numbers, we must label $10, 12, \cdots, 98$ as $5, 6, \cdots, 49$ by dividing the original sequence by 2. Then, subtract 4 from each number to come up with a sequence of $1, 2, \cdots, 45$. Since all three sequences have one-to-one correspondence, we conclude there are 45 numbers in two-digit even numbers. Now, move onto 4-digit numbers. In particular, turn $1000, 1002, 1004, \cdots, 1108$ into $500, 501, 502, \cdots, 554$, which is equal to $46, 47, 48, \cdots, 100$. As one can see from three layers of numbers, the last layer indiciates the position of the number in ordered sequence from smallest to largest, and the middle layer indicates the number divided by 2 from the original sequence. Hence, by one-to-one correspondence, we end up getting 1108. The sum of its digits equals $1 + 1 + 0 + 8 = 10$.

5. (A)

First five odd single-digit numbers use up 5 numbers. Hence, 101 must be 6th number. We must count 100th number in the list. Similar to the previous question, we use equal strategy of using one-to-one correspondence. Turn $101, 103, 105, \cdots, 289$ into $100, 102, 104, \cdots, 288$. Turn it into $50, 51, 52, \cdots, 144$, which in turn equals $6, 7, 8, \cdots, 100$. As shown above, 289 is the 100th positive odd integer with odd number of digits. Hence, the sum of digits of 289 equals $2 + 8 + 9 = 19$.

6. (E)

We use the idea of complementary counting. Imagine that every element of a sequence is 2. Then, the sum must have been 2×50. However, if i is a power of 2, then $x_i = 1$. In other words, we added more at x_2, x_4, x_8, x_{16} and x_{32}. In other words, we must subtract 5 from 100. Therefore, the sum of all elements in the sequence equals 95.

7. (E)

Notice that 0 cannot be in the first position of the four-digit number. So, we begin with a number that starts with 1. Since 0, 2, and 3 are arranged from least to greatest in the three boxes, there are 3! ways of arranging them. Hence, the 7th term must be 2013. Likewise, a number that starts with 2 has 3! ways of arranging 0, 1 and 3. Hence, the 13th term is 3012. Thus, the difference between 3012 and 2013 is 999.

8. (D)

Let's find out triangular numbers less than or equal to 2021. In particular,

$$T_n = 1 + 2 + 3 + \cdots + n$$
$$= \frac{n(n+1)}{2}$$
$$< 2021$$

at $n \leq 63$. Hence, there are 63 triangular numbers in the list. As if we are using the complementary counting method, consider all elements in the sequence as 1, so the sum turns out to be 2021. In order to make the element at triangular number -1, we need to subtract 2 by 63 number of times. Hence, $2021 - 2(63) = 1895$. The sum of the digits equals $23 = 1 + 8 + 9 + 5$.

9. (B)

$$T_1 = 1$$
$$T_2 = 3$$
$$T_3 = 6$$
$$T_4 = 10$$
$$T_5 = 15$$
$$T_6 = 21$$
$$T_7 = 28$$
$$T_8 = 36$$
$$T_9 = 45$$
$$T_{10} = 55$$
$$\vdots = \vdots$$

By pure observation using parities, one can notice that triangular numbers' parities have cycles of "odd, odd, even, even." Since $T_{63} = 2016$ is the greatest triangular number less than or equal to 2021, divide 63 by 4 to count that there are 15 bundles of perfect cycles and three additional terms that do not make a full cycle. Hence, there are 30 even numbers in 15 bundles of cycles, and 1 even term, i.e., $T_{63} = 2016$. Thus, there are 31 even numbers.

10. (C)
Let $1936 = (k+16)^2$ by using one-to-one correspondence. Using the given condition of strictly increasing or decreasing order, we conclude that $k + 16 = \pm 44$, so $k = -60$ or $k = 28$. Hence, the sum of these two values equals -32. In particular, there are two possible set arrangements.

$$\begin{cases} \{(-60)^2, (-59)^2, \cdots, (-44)^2\} \\ \{(28)^2, (29)^2, \cdots, 44^2\} \end{cases}$$

Hence, there are two possible arrangements of a set, and a set is not necessarily ordered one, so we must think about the two possibilities, i.e., when $k = -60$ and $k = 28$.

11. (C)

We will use De Morgan's Law. Given two sets A and B, $A^c \cap B^c = (A \cup B)^c$. Since the total number of arrangements of five subjects to five people is 5!, we get 120. Now, we need to compute A, the case when the first person chooses History; B, the case when the last person chooses Math. Hence, $|A| = 4!$ since four people must choose the remaining four subjects. Likewise, $|B| = 4!$, using the same reasoning. Now, $|A \cap B| = 3!$, since the first and last person have chosen their specific subjects and there are three people to decide which subject to choose out of three subjects. Hence,
$|A^c \cap B^c| = 120 - |(A \cup B)| = 120 - (2 \cdot 4! - 3!) = 78$.

12. (E)

We will use De Morgan's Law as well. $A^c \cup B^c = (A \cap B)^c$. Since we know that $|A \cap B| = 3! = 6$, we use the complementary counting method to get $|A^c \cup B^c| = 120 - 6 = 114$.

13. (C)

This uses the essence of De Morgan's Law. Let G be the set of mathletes taking Geometry, C be the set of mathletes taking Combinatorics, and N be the set of mathletes taking Number Theory. Then, $|G^c| = 50$, $|C^c| = 30$, and $|N^c| = 20$. Since $|G \cap C \cap N| = 0$, and $(G \cap C \cap N)^c = G^c \cup C^c \cup N^c$, by De Morgan's Law, we can conclude that G^c, C^c and N^c are all disjoint sets. Now, we need to compute $|C \cap G|$. Using De Morgan's Law, $(C \cap G)^c = C^c \cup G^c = 50 + 30 = 80$. Hence, $|C \cap G| = 100 - 80 = 20$.

14. (C)

Let x be the number of people using all three. Then, according to the given condition, the number of people who are using flat bench only equals $40 - x$, that of people who are using power rack equals $15 - x$, and that of people who are using barbells equals $30 - x$. Hence, the total number of people must be equal to
$(40 - x) + (15 - x) + (30 - x) + 30 + 40 + 25 + x = 180 - 2x = 150$. Hence, $180 - 2x = 150$ implies that $x = 15$.

15. (D)

Let A, B, C, and D be the set of kids who like doing activities in the order written in the question. Then, $|A^c| = 40$, $|B^c| = 30$, $|C^c| = 20$ and $|D^c| = 10$. Since $A^c \cup B^c \cup C^c \cup D^c = 100$, we know that each complement is disjoint with one another. Now, we need to compute $|A \cap C|$. By De Morgan's Law, $A^c \cup C^c = (A \cap C)^c$, and $|A^c \cup C^c| = 60$, so $|A \cap C| = 40$.

16. (B)

Let O be the set of kids having watched Octonauts, and P be the set of kids having watched Peppa Pig. Then, $|O^c \cap P^c| = |(O \cup P)^c| = 3$ implies that $|O \cup P| = 27$. Since $|P| = 2|O|$, notice that $|P \cup O| = |P| + |O| - |P \cap O| = 3|O| - 3 = 27$. Therefore, $|O| = 10$. This implies that $|P| = 20$. The number of kids who only watched Peppa Pig is equal to $|P \cap O^c| = |P| - |P \cap O| = 20 - 3 = 17$.

17. (D)

Each of the term in the expansion must have a look of $x_i y_j z_k$ for some $1 \leq i \leq 4$, $1 \leq j \leq 3$, and $1 \leq k \leq 4$. Hence, there are $4 \times 3 \times 4 = 48$ number of distinct terms in the expansion by the principle of multiplication.

18. (C)

Each of the term in the expansion must have a look of $x_i y_j z_k$ for some $1 \leq i \leq 4$, $1 \leq j \leq 3$, and $1 \leq k \leq 4$. Now, it is time for us to casework. The first case is when all the indices are even. Then, $i \in \{2, 4\}$, $j \in \{2\}$ and $k \in \{2, 4\}$, so there are 4 possible cases. The second case is when two of the indices are odd and the remaining one is even. Then, there are three subcases.

- $(i, j, k) = (o, o, e) : 2 \times 2 \times 2$ different arrangements.
- $(i, j, k) = (o, e, o) : 2 \times 1 \times 2$ different arrangements.
- $(i, j, k) = (e, o, o) : 2 \times 2 \times 2$ different arrangements.

Hence, there are $24 = 4 + 8 + 4 + 8$ different terms whose sum of indices is even.

19. (C)

This is a typical casework question. Let $x = 1$. Then, $2y + z = 17$ at $(y, z) = (8, 1), (7, 3)$, $\cdots, (1, 15)$. Let $x = 2$. Then, $2y + z = 14$ at $(y, z) = (6, 2), \cdots, (1, 12)$. Let $x = 3$. Then, $2y + z = 11$ at $(y, z) = (5, 1), (4, 3), \cdots, (1, 9)$. Let $x = 4$. Then, $2y + z = 8$ at $(y, z) = (3, 2), (2, 4), (1, 6)$. Let $x = 5$. Then, $2y + z = 5$ at $(y, z) = (2, 1)$ and $(1, 3)$. Hence, total number of tuples must be $24 (= 8 + 6 + 5 + 3 + 2)$.

20. (E)

First, let grandparents choose their rows by 2 ways. Then, the grandfather can choose his seat in three ways, and so can she. There are four seats left for three grandchildren to choose. Hence,

$$2! \times 3 \times 3 \times 4 \times 3 \times 2 = 432$$

21. (A)

We can easily find out that the solution tuples are

$$(x, y, z) = (1, 8, 1)$$
$$= (1, 7, 3)$$
$$= (1, 6, 5)$$
$$= (1, 5, 7)$$
$$= (1, 4, 9)$$
$$= (1, 3, 11)$$
$$= (1, 2, 13)$$
$$= (1, 1, 15)$$
$$= (2, 6, 2)$$
$$= (2, 5, 4)$$
$$= (2, 4, 6)$$
$$= (2, 3, 8)$$
$$= (2, 2, 10)$$
$$= (2, 1, 12)$$
$$= (3, 5, 1)$$
$$= (3, 4, 3)$$
$$= (3, 3, 5)$$
$$= (3, 2, 7)$$
$$= (3, 1, 9)$$
$$= (4, 3, 2)$$
$$= (4, 2, 4)$$
$$= (4, 1, 6)$$
$$= (5, 2, 1)$$
$$= (5, 1, 3)$$

Therefore, there are only 9 tuples satisfying $x \leq y \leq z$, i.e., $(1, 5, 7)$, $(1, 4, 9)$, $(1, 3, 11)$, $(1, 2, 13)$, $(1, 1, 15)$, $(2, 4, 6)$, $(2, 3, 8)$, $(2, 2, 10)$, and $(3, 3, 5)$.

22. (B)

For both Bob and Bo, we choose colors for a pair of socks and shoes in two ways each. Now, Bob can choose one out of three kinds of socks and shoes, and Bo can choose the rest. Hence,
$$2^2 \times 3 \times 2 \times 3 \times 2 = 144$$

23. (C)

Let A be the set of arrangements where one of the columns is placed with I and 1. Let B be the set of arrangements where one of the columns is placed with II and 2. Let C be the set of arrangements where one of the columns is placed with III and 3. Let D be the set of arrangements where one of the columns is placed with IV and 4. Since we are looking for $|A^c \cap B^c \cap C^c \cap D^c|$, we must look at the complementary sets by using the principle of inclusion and exclusion. This is also known as "derangement," which can be computed by
$$\frac{4!}{0!} - \frac{4!}{1!} + \frac{4!}{2!} - \frac{4!}{3!} + \frac{4!}{4!} = 12 - 4 + 1 = 9$$

24. (A)

In total, there are $3 \times 2 \times 2 \times 2 \times 2 \times 2 = 96$ ways of possible paths. Now, we need to eliminate the paths that come back to P, which can be counted by 6 different paths. Hence, using complementary counting, we can eliminate 6 from 96 to conclude that there are 90 different paths that can be traced after six moves.

25. (D)

Let's perform casework. If there is one athlete in the volleyball team, then there are $4 \times 2^3 = 32$ ways of dividing a group of four athletes. If there are two athletes in the volleyball team, then there are $\frac{4 \times 3}{2 \times 1} \times 2^2 = 24$ ways of dividing a group of four athletes. If there are three athletes in the volleyball team, then there are $\frac{4 \times 3 \times 2}{3 \times 2 \times 1} \times 2 = 8$ ways of dividing a group of four athletes. If there are four athletes in the volleyball team, then there is $\frac{4 \times 3 \times 2 \times 1}{4 \times 3 \times 2 \times 1} = 1$ way of dividing a group of four athletes. Hence, there are 65 ways of dividing a group of four people satisfying the given condition.

26. (C)

There are two possible cases to cover. The first is when $x < y < z$. The number of (x, y, z) equals the number of choosing three different integers from a set $\{1, 2, 3, 4, \cdots, 10\}$. The second is when $x = y < z$. The number of (x, y, z) equals the number of choosing two different integers from a set $\{1, 2, 3, \cdots, 10\}$. Therefore,
$$\frac{10 \times 9 \times 8}{3 \times 2 \times 1} + \frac{10 \times 9}{2 \times 1} = 120 + 45 = 165$$

27. (C)

There are four possible cases to cover. If $x < y < z$, then we choose three elements out of five numbers. Likewise, if $x = y < z$, then we choose two elements out of five elements. If $x < y = z$, then we choose two elements out of five elements. If $x = y = z$, then we choose one element out of five. Hence,

$$\frac{5 \times 4 \times 3}{3 \times 2 \times 1} + \frac{5 \times 4}{2 \times 1} + \frac{5 \times 4}{2 \times 1} + 5 = 10 + 10 + 10 + 5 = 35$$

28. (C)

We must perform casework on the last two digits. If the last two digits are 12, then we must arrange 3, 3, 4, and 5. If the last two digits are 24, then we must arrange 1, 3, 3, and 5. If the last two digits are 32, then we must arrange 1, 3, 4, and 5. If the last two digits are 52, the we must arrange 1, 3, 3, and 4. Hence,

$$\frac{4!}{2!} + \frac{4!}{2!} + 4! + \frac{4!}{2!} = 12 + 12 + 24 + 12 = 60$$

29. (A)

Given two circles apart, there are four tangent lines to draw. Now, we must count how many two circles can be chosen out of five circles. Since there are infinitely many lines tangent to a circle, we exclude all those cases, except the lines that are tangent to two circles. Hence,

$$\frac{5 \times 4}{2 \times 1} \times 4 = 40$$

30. (C)

Let's assume that $x + y + z = 12$ where $x \geq y \geq z$. Then, by translation property, $12 < 3x$. On the other hand, by triangular inequality, $2x \leq 12$, so $x \leq 6$. According to this bound, we produce two cases. The first is when $x = 4$. Then, $y + z = 8$ where $4 \geq y \geq z$. There is only one solution $(y, z) = (4, 4)$. The second is when $x = 5$. Then, $y + z = 7$ where $5 \geq y \geq z$. There are two solutions $(y, z) = (5, 2), (4, 3)$. Hence, there are three distinct triangles.

31. (D)

Let $\overline{ABC}$ be a three-digit number satisfying the original condition. Then, $2B = A + C$. Let's perform caseworks.

- $B = 1$ implies $(A, C) = (2, 0), (1, 1)$.

- $B = 2$ implies $(A, C) = (4, 0), (3, 1), (2, 2), (1, 3)$.

- $B = 3$ implies $(A, C) = (6, 0), (5, 1), \cdots, (1, 5)$.

- $B = 4$ implies $(A, C) = (8, 0), (7, 1), \cdots, (1, 7)$.

- $B = 5$ implies $(A, C) = (9, 1), (8, 2), \cdots, (1, 9)$.
- $B = 6$ implies $(A, C) = (9, 3), (8, 4), \cdots, (3, 9)$.
- $B = 7$ implies $(A, C) = (9, 5), (8, 6), \cdots, (5, 9)$.
- $B = 8$ implies $(A, C) = (9, 7), (8, 8), (7, 9)$.
- $B = 9$ implies $(A, C) = (9, 9)$.

Then, there are 45 number of such integers.

32. (B)

There are three places for bars to be placed. In particular, if we label the spots with x_1, $x_2, \cdots, x_9$, then the bars can be at (x_1, x_4, x_7), (x_2, x_5, x_8), and (x_3, x_6, x_9). All the other places must be filled with six numbers, so

$$3 \times 3! \times 6! = 3 \times 6 \times 720 = 12960$$

Hence, $n = 12960$, so $n/10 = 1296$.

33. (A)

Make Bob sit on any seat around the table. Then, Bo can be seated in one possible way. Now, let others be seated, so

$$1 \times 1 \times 4! = 24$$

Hence, there are 24 possible ways to make six people be seated around the circle satisfying the given condition.

34. (A)

There are three possible seats for Bob to choose. As soon as Bob sits, Bo's seat is automatically set. Hence, the number of arrangements of twelve people can be computed as

$$3 \times 1 \times 10! = 10886400$$

There are 8 digits in total.

35. (A)

Let's use complementary counting. Label the position of water stations from 1 to 9. Let's first count the number of cases when all three seats are adjacent, i.e., $(1, 2, 3), (2, 3, 4), \cdots$, $(9, 1, 2)$. Now, let's count the number of cases when only two seats are adjacent.

- $(1, 2, x)$ where $x = 4, 5, 6, 7, 8$.
- $(2, 3, x)$ where $x = 5, 6, 7, 8, 9$.

- $(3, 4, x)$ where $x = 6, 7, 8, 9, 1$.

- $(4, 5, x)$ where $x = 7, 8, 9, 1, 2$.

- $(5, 6, x)$ where $x = 8, 9, 1, 2, 3$.

- $(7, 8, x)$ where $x = 1, 2, 3, 4, 5$.

- $(8, 9, x)$ where $x = 2, 3, 4, 5, 6$.

- $(9, 1, x)$ where $x = 3, 4, 5, 6, 7$.

Hence, we compute the answer by using complementary counting, i.e.,

$$\frac{9 \times 8 \times 7}{3 \times 2 \times 1} - 9 - 45 = 84 - 54 = 30$$

36. (B)
First, choose a rectangle by drawing two horizontal lines and two vertical lines. Then, multiply by 4 since there are 4 right triangles associated to each rectangle. Therefore, there are

$$\frac{4 \times 3}{2 \times 1} \times \frac{4 \times 3}{2 \times 1} \times 4 = 144$$

right triangles.

37. (E)
Let's label a row of chairs by numbers from 1 to 8. Then, $(1, 3, 5)$, $(1, 3, 6)$, $(1, 3, 7)$, $(1, 3, 8)$, $(1, 4, 6)$, $(1, 4, 7)$, $(1, 4, 8)$, $(1, 5, 7)$, $(1, 5, 8)$, $(1, 6, 8)$, $(2, 4, 6)$, $(2, 4, 7)$, $(2, 4, 8)$, $(2, 5, 7)$, $(2, 5, 8)$, $(2, 6, 8)$, $(3, 5, 7)$, $(3, 5, 8)$, $(3, 6, 8)$, $(4, 6, 8)$ are the only seats that Ann, Ben, and Dan can sit. Hence, there are

$$20 \times 3! = 120$$

possible ways for them to be seated.

38. (C)
First, there is an identity function. Second, choose two elements (a, b) such that $f(a) = b$ and $f(b) = a$. Third, make such two-element partition twice, i.e., $\{a, b\}, \{c, d\}$. Hence, there are

$$1 + \frac{4 \times 3}{2 \times 1} + \frac{4 \times 3}{2 \times 1} \cdot \frac{2 \times 1}{2 \times 1} \cdot \frac{1}{2!} = 1 + 6 + 3 = 10$$

39. (E)

If a cat is seated, then we may have (F, C, M) or (M, C, F) where M is a male adult and F is a female adult. Since there are no other restrictions than this, we compute the total number of arrangements as
$$2 \times 2 \times 2 \times 2! = 16$$

40. (A)

Consider five black marbles as five natural numbers, and white marbles as "+" symbol. In other words, we could partition 5 into three whole numbers such that

$$5 + 0 + 0 = 5$$
$$4 + 1 + 0 = 5$$
$$3 + 2 + 0 = 5$$
$$3 + 1 + 1 = 5$$
$$2 + 2 + 1 = 5$$

Now, $(5, 0, 0)$ is equivalent to $(0, 5, 0)$ and $(0, 0, 5)$. On the other hand, $(4, 1, 0)$ is distinct from $(4, 0, 1)$, though circular permutation is allowed. Likewise, $(3, 2, 0)$ is distinct from $(3, 0, 2)$. However, $(3, 1, 1)$ and $(2, 2, 1)$ are equivalent to $(1, 3, 1)$, $(1, 1, 3)$, $(2, 1, 2)$, and $(1, 2, 2)$ respectively. Hence, there are

$$1 + 2 + 2 + 1 + 1 = 7$$

possible arrangements of eight marbles around a circle.

TOPIC 2

Distinguishables and Indistinguishables

2.1　Partition of Natural Numbers

Partition of natural numbers is used mostly to find out the total number of case enumerations, in both number theory and combinatorics. Instead of going over a formula, it would be better to provide with a general rule for partition of natural numbers. We can also look at partition of natural numbers as allocating

$$\underline{\text{Indistinguishable}}\text{ marbles} \longrightarrow \underline{\text{Indistinguishable}}\text{ plates}$$

where "indistinguishable" means the state where objects are unordered. In particular, we find the number of ways by the following rules.

- We first "lock" the order.
- Go through every single case until we reach a deadend, then move to other cases.

Example Partition 5 into three whole numbers.

Step-by-step Solution

#1. Let a, b, and c be whole numbers such that $a + b + c = 5$.
#2. We lock the order, i.e., $a \geq b \geq c$.
#3. Then,

$$a + b + c = 5$$
$$5 + 0 + 0 = 5$$
$$4 + 1 + 0 = 5$$
$$3 + 2 + 0 = 5$$
$$3 + 1 + 1 = 5$$
$$2 + 2 + 1 = 5$$

Example Partition 6 into three natural numbers.

Step-by-step Solution

#1. Let a, b, and c be whole numbers such that $a + b + c = 6$.
#2. We lock the order, i.e., $a \geq b \geq c \geq 1$.
#3. Then,

$$a + b + c = 6$$
$$4 + 1 + 1 = 6$$
$$3 + 2 + 1 = 6$$
$$2 + 2 + 2 = 6$$

2.2 Partition of Sets

When there are some people or distinct objects that should be partitioned, we use parition of sets. In fact, we may look at partition of sets as allocating

$$\underline{\text{Distinguishable}} \text{ marbles} \longrightarrow \underline{\text{Indistinguishable}} \text{ plates}$$

- Perform caseworks, using partition of natural numbers.
- Partition sets, making sure there are no overcounts.

Example Compute the number of partitioning 5 students into three groups with at least one member.

Step-by-step Solution

#1. Let α, β, and γ be whole numbers such that $\alpha + \beta + \gamma = 5$.
#2. We lock the order, i.e., $\alpha \geq \beta \geq \gamma \geq 1$.
#3. Then,

$$\alpha + \beta + \gamma = 5$$
$$3 + 1 + 1 = 5$$
$$2 + 2 + 1 = 5$$

#4. For $(\alpha, \beta, \gamma) = (3, 1, 1)$, we partition five people into $\binom{5}{3} \times \binom{2}{1} \times \binom{1}{1} \times \frac{1}{2!} = 10$ ways.
#5. For $(\alpha, \beta, \gamma) = (2, 2, 1)$, we partition five people into $\binom{5}{2} \times \binom{3}{2} \times \binom{1}{1} \times \frac{1}{2!} = 15$ ways.
#6. The reason why we divide by 2! is that two groups with same number of elements are overcounted in the previous step. For instance, $\{a, b, c\}, \{e\}, \{d\}$ should be considered equal to $\{a, b, c\}, \{d\}, \{e\}$. Hence, in #4, we divide the count by 2!. Likewise, $\{a, b\}, \{c, d\}, \{e\}$ should be considered equal to $\{c, d\}, \{a, b\}, \{e\}$. Hence, in #5, we divide the count by 2!.

Example Find the number of partitioning 6 people into three groups with at least one member, each of which has distinct number of members.

Step-by-step Solution

#1. Let a, b, and c be whole numbers such that $a + b + c = 6$ satisfying $a \geq b \geq c \geq 1$.
#2. Then, $a + b + c = 6$ has a single solution $3 + 2 + 1 = 6$.
#3. Hence, the answer is $\binom{6}{3} \times \binom{3}{2} \times \binom{1}{1} = 60$.

2.3 Permutation allowing Repetition

Permutation allowing repetition goes a bit further than the partition of sets. In other words, a set with distinct objects may be partitioned first, then we distribute these objects into relative places. In fact, we may consider permutation allowing repetition as allocating

$$\underline{\text{Distinguishable}} \text{ marbles} \longrightarrow \underline{\text{Distinguishable}} \text{ plates}$$

Example Compute the number of distributing 5 students into three clubs - math, history, and debate - with at least one member.

Step-by-step Solution

#1. As we already did in previous section, we perform partition of sets, i.e.,

$$a + b + c = 5$$
$$3 + 1 + 1 = 5$$
$$2 + 2 + 1 = 5$$

#2. For $(a, b, c) = (3, 1, 1)$, we partition five students into $\binom{5}{3} \times \binom{2}{1} \times \binom{1}{1} \times \frac{1}{2!} = 10$ ways. Now, distribute these three groups into three distinct clubs by multiplying $3!$. Hence, there are 60 ways.

#3. For $(a, b, c) = (2, 2, 1)$, we partition five students into $\binom{5}{2} \times \binom{3}{2} \times \binom{1}{1} \times \frac{1}{2!} = 15$ ways. Now, distribute these three groups into three distinct clubs by multiplying $3!$. Hence, there are 90 ways.

#4. In total, there are 150 number of ways to distributing five students into three distinct clubs, satisfying the given condition.

If the problem above has no restriction about the number of members in each group, then we can consider it as a typical permutation allowing repetition, whose answer is in the form of n^p for some integers n and p.

Example Compute the number of distributing 5 students into three clubs - math, history, and debate - with the assumption of that there could be no one in some groups.

Step-by-step Solution

#1. This is a typical permutation allowing repetition. The first student has three choices to make. The second student also has three choices to make. The third, fourth and last student also have three choices to make, respectively.

#2. Hence, there are $3^5 = 243$ number of ways to distribute 5 students into three clubs.

2.4 Combination allowing Repetition

Combination allowing repetition, similar to permutation allowing repetition, goes a bit further than partition of natural numbers. In other words, we put "order" to each case found in the partition of natural numbers. In fact, we may look at combination allowing repetitions as allocating

$$\underline{\text{Indistinguishable}} \text{ marbles} \longrightarrow \underline{\text{Distinguishable}} \text{ plates}$$

Example In how many ways can 5 identical-looking marbles be placed into three distinct bundles, assuming there could be at least one bundle containing no marble?

Step-by-step Solution

#1. We must partition 5, i.e.,

$$a + b + c = 5$$
$$5 + 0 + 0 = 5$$
$$4 + 1 + 0 = 5$$
$$3 + 2 + 0 = 5$$
$$3 + 1 + 1 = 5$$
$$2 + 2 + 1 = 5$$

#2. Now, we make an order to each of the cases. $(5,0,0)$ has three cases. $(4,1,0)$ has six cases. $(3,2,0)$ has six cases. $(3,1,1)$ has three cases, and $(2,2,1)$ has three cases.

#3. Hence, there are $3 + 6 + 6 + 3 + 3 = 21$ number of ways to place 5 identical-looking marbles into three distinct bundles.

Instead of rearranging each case found in partition of natural numbers, we may use "circles and bars." The 5 we see on the right side of the equation can be considered as 5 circles, and we put two bars in the place of + signs.

$$5 + 0 + 0 \longleftrightarrow \bigcirc\bigcirc\bigcirc\bigcirc\bigcirc//$$
$$4 + 1 + 0 \longleftrightarrow \bigcirc\bigcirc\bigcirc\bigcirc/\bigcirc/$$
$$3 + 2 + 0 \longleftrightarrow \bigcirc\bigcirc\bigcirc/\bigcirc\bigcirc/$$
$$3 + 1 + 1 \longleftrightarrow \bigcirc\bigcirc\bigcirc/\bigcirc/\bigcirc$$
$$2 + 2 + 1 \longleftrightarrow \bigcirc\bigcirc/\bigcirc\bigcirc/\bigcirc$$

In other words, we are permuting five circles and two bars in $\binom{7}{2} = 21$ ways.

Practice

1. $(6,2,1,1)$ is one possible partition of 10 into four natural numbers, since $6+2+1+1=10$. Compute the number of partition of 10 into 4 natural numbers.

(A) 5 (B) 7 (C) 9 (D) 11 (E) 13

2. $(7,1,1,1)$ is one possible partition of 10 into four odd whole numbers. Compute the number of partition of 10 into 4 odd whole numbers.

(A) 1 (B) 3 (C) 5 (D) 7 (E) 9

3. $(6,2,2,0)$ is one possible partition of 10 into four even whole numbers. Compute the number of partition of 10 into 4 even whole numbers.

(A) 2   (B) 4   (C) 6   (D) 8   (E) 10

4. $(5,4,1,0)$ is one of the partitions of 10 into four whole numbers, in descending order, such that it is written in alternating parities starting from odd and ending with even, i.e., (odd, even,odd,even). Compute the number of partition of 10 satisfying this parity-changing condition that starts with odd.

(A) 1   (B) 2   (C) 3   (D) 4   (E) 5

5. Compute the number of paritions of 5 people into at most three indistinguishable groups.

(A) 38   (B) 39   (C) 40   (D) 41   (E) 42

6. Compute the number of paritions of 8 people into three indistinguishable groups, assuming that there are at least one person in each group and the number of people in each group is distinct.

(A) 400   (B) 441   (C) 448   (D) 462   (E) 525

7. There are 6 athletes in an ice hockey team. The coach has 2 jerseys in each of 3 colors to mark 3 teams for practice. How many ways can he give out the jerseys? Assume that jerseys of the same color are indistinguishable.

(A) 90   (B) 100   (C) 110   (D) 120   (E) 130

8. There are 8 soldiers in a squad, further grouped into two teams of equal fire functionalities with four men each. In how many different ways will a squad consist of the two teams, where each team has a team leader?

(A) 120   (B) 240   (C) 360   (D) 480   (E) 560

9. How many distinguishable ways are there to write 10 as the sum of 2's and 4's, where the order of the addends matters? For example, $4+4+2$ and $2+4+4$ are two different ways.

(A) 3 (B) 5 (C) 8 (D) 10 (E) 13

10. Given $\Omega = \{1, 2, 3, 4, 5\}$, there are two subsets X and Y such that $X \subset \Omega$ and $Y \subset \Omega$. If $Y \cap X^c = \{2, 5\}$, where X^c is the set of elements in Ω such that every element in X^c does not belong to X, compute the number of distinct pairs of (X, Y).

(A) 12 (B) 18 (C) 21 (D) 24 (E) 27

11. Given $\Omega = \{1, 2, 3, 4, 5\}$, there are two subsets X and Y such that $X \subset \Omega$ and $Y \subset \Omega$. If $|Y \cap X^c| = 3$, where X^c is the set of elements in Ω such that every element in X^c does not belong to X, compute the number of distinct pairs of (X, Y).

(A) 90 (B) 100 (C) 110 (D) 120 (E) 130

12. How many ways are there to put 5 distinct marbles into 3 distinguishable boxes, assuming that there should be at least one marble in each box?

(A) 90 (B) 120 (C) 150 (D) 180 (E) 210

13. How many ways are there to put 5 indistinct marbles into 3 distinguishable boxes?

(A) 20 (B) 21 (C) 45 (D) 81 (E) 100

14. How many ways are there to put 5 indistinct marbles into 3 distinguishable boxes, assuming that there should be at least one marble in each box?

(A) 3 (B) 4 (C) 5 (D) 6 (E) 7

15. If a, b, and c are integers such that $1 \leq a \leq b \leq c \leq 4$, compute the number of distinct triples of (a, b, c).

(A) 20 (B) 21 (C) 45 (D) 81 (E) 100

16. If a, b, and c are integers such that $2|2^a|2^b|2^c|32$, where $x|y$ means y is divisible by x, compute the number of distinct triples of (a, b, c).

(A) 20 (B) 25 (C) 35 (D) 56 (E) 84

17. Let x, y, and z be non-negative integers. Compute the number of distinct triples (x, y, z) satisfying $x + y + z \leq 5$.

(A) 45   (B) 56   (C) 63   (D) 81   (E) 99

18. If the product of integers a, b, and c equals 7^n, where n is a positive integer, then there are 312 number of distinct triples satisfying the given condition. Which of the following is equal to the value of n?

(A) 10   (B) 11   (C) 12   (D) 13   (E) 14

19. Given a set $\{1, 2, 3, 4, \cdots, 10\}$, compute the number of 4-element subsets such that any consecutive pair, when ordered from least to greatest, has the difference of at least 2.

(A) 35   (B) 46   (C) 53   (D) 71   (E) 89

20. How many ordered triples (a, b, c) of odd positive integers satisfy $a + b + c = 31$?

(A) 100   (B) 110   (C) 120   (D) 130   (E) 140

Solution

1. (C)

When you see the word "partition," then we usually "lock" the order between a, b, c, and d. In particular, we would like to put an order $a \geq b \geq c \geq d$. Now, use the partition of natural numbers to come up with

$$a + b + c + d = 10$$
$$7 + 1 + 1 + 1 = 10$$
$$6 + 2 + 1 + 1 = 10$$
$$5 + 3 + 1 + 1 = 10$$
$$4 + 4 + 1 + 1 = 10$$
$$5 + 2 + 2 + 1 = 10$$
$$4 + 3 + 2 + 1 = 10$$
$$3 + 3 + 3 + 1 = 10$$
$$4 + 2 + 2 + 2 = 10$$
$$3 + 3 + 2 + 2 = 10$$

Hence, there are nine partitions of 10 satisfying the given condition.

2. (B)

We lock the order between a, b, c, and d, by $a \geq b \geq c \geq d$. Now, we use one-to-one correspondence idea to come up with $a = 2a' + 1$, $b = 2b' + 1$, $c = 2c' + 1$, and $d = 2d' + 1$ where $a' \geq b' \geq c' \geq d' \geq 0$, still maintaining the order that we "lock"ed in the previous step. Now, use the partition of natural numbers to come up with

$$a + b + c + d = 10$$
$$(2a' + 1) + (2b' + 1) + (2c' + 1) + (2d' + 1) = 10$$
$$2a' + 2b' + 2c' + 2d' = 6$$
$$a' + b' + c' + d' = 3$$
$$3 + 0 + 0 + 0 = 3$$
$$2 + 1 + 0 + 0 = 3$$
$$1 + 1 + 1 + 0 = 3$$

Hence, there are three partitions of 10 satisfying the given condition.

3. (C)

We lock the order between a, b, c, and d, by $a \geq b \geq c \geq d$. Now, we use one-to-one correspondence idea to come up with $a = 2a'$, $b = 2b'$, $c = 2c'$, and $d = 2d'$ where $a' \geq b' \geq c' \geq d' \geq 0$, still maintaining the order that we "lock"ed in the previous step. Use the partition of natural numbers to come up with

$$a + b + c + d = 10$$
$$2a' + 2b' + 2c' + 2d' = 10$$
$$a' + b' + c' + d' = 5$$
$$5 + 0 + 0 + 0 = 5$$
$$4 + 1 + 0 + 0 = 5$$
$$3 + 2 + 0 + 0 = 5$$
$$3 + 1 + 1 + 0 = 5$$
$$2 + 2 + 1 + 0 = 5$$
$$2 + 1 + 1 + 1 = 5$$

Hence, there are six partitions of 10 satisfying the given condition.

4. (B)

We lock the order between a, b, c, and d, by $a \geq b \geq c \geq d$. Now, we use one-to-one correspondence idea to come up with $a = 2a' + 3$, $b = 2b' + 2$, $c = 2c' + 1$, and $d = 2d'$ where $a' \geq b' \geq c' \geq d' \geq 0$, still maintaining the order that we "lock"ed in the previous step and the condition of alternating parities. Use the partition of natural numbers to come up with

$$a + b + c + d = 10$$
$$(2a' + 3) + (2b' + 2) + (2c' + 1) + 2d' = 10$$
$$2(a' + b' + c' + d') + 6 = 10$$
$$2(a' + b' + c' + d') = 4$$
$$a' + b' + c' + d' = 2$$
$$2 + 0 + 0 + 0 = 2$$
$$1 + 1 + 0 + 0 = 2$$

Hence, there are two possible cases of (a, b, c, d) satisfying the given partition condition.

5. (D)

Use the partition of natural numbers to come up with

$$a + b + c = 5$$
$$5 + 0 + 0 = 5$$
$$4 + 1 + 0 = 5$$
$$3 + 2 + 0 = 5$$
$$3 + 1 + 1 = 5$$
$$2 + 2 + 1 = 5$$

Hence, we get five different possible cases to cover. Therefore,

$$\binom{5}{5} + \binom{5}{4} \times \binom{1}{1} + \binom{5}{3} \times \binom{2}{2} + \binom{5}{3} \times \binom{2}{1} \times \binom{1}{1} \times \frac{1}{2!} + \binom{5}{2} \times \binom{3}{2} \times \binom{1}{1} \times \frac{1}{2!}$$
$$= 1 + 5 + 10 + 10 + 15$$
$$= 41$$

number of partition of 5 people satisfying the given condition.

6. (C)

Use the parition of natural numbers to come up with

$$a + b + c = 8$$
$$5 + 2 + 1 = 8$$
$$4 + 3 + 1 = 8$$

Hence, we get two possible cases to cover. Therefore,

$$\binom{8}{5} \times \binom{3}{2} \times \binom{1}{1} + \binom{8}{4} \times \binom{4}{3} \times \binom{1}{1} = 168 + 280 = 448$$

number of partition of 8 people satisfying the given condition.

7. (A)

First, partition 6 people into three groups such that each group has two members each. Then, distribute three different colors to the partitioned team. Hence, the coach can give jerseys in

$$\binom{6}{2} \times \binom{4}{2} \times \binom{2}{2} \times \frac{1}{3!} \times 3! = 90$$

ways to six different athletes.

8. (E)

First, divide eight people into two groups of four men. Then, choose a team leader in each team. There are
$$\binom{8}{4} \times \binom{4}{4} \times \frac{1}{2!} \times \binom{4}{1} \times \binom{4}{1} = 560$$
different ways to do so.

9. (C)

Use a strategy similar to partition of natural numbers to conclude

$$\begin{aligned} 10 &= 4 + 4 + 2 \\ &= 4 + 2 + 2 + 2 \\ &= 2 + 2 + 2 + 2 + 2 \end{aligned}$$

Now, $(4, 4, 2)$ has $\binom{3}{1}$ ways to rearrange. $(4, 2, 2, 2)$ has $\binom{4}{1}$ ways to rearrange. $(2, 2, 2, 2, 2)$ has $\binom{5}{5}$ ways to rearrange. Hence, there are 8 different ways to write 10 as the sum of 2's and 4's, where the order of addends matters.

10. (E)

This is a typical problem related to permutation allowing repetition. First, there is a unique one-to-one correspondence between the number of distinct pairs of (X, Y) and the assignment of each element in Venn Diagram such that $Y \cap X^c = \{2, 5\}$. Hence, we must assign 1 into either $Y \cap X$, $X \cap Y^c$, or $(X \cup Y)^c$. There are three possible disjoint sets for its assignment. We have exactly same number of disjoint sets for 3 and 4. Hence, there are 3^3 number of ways to assign 1, 3, and 4 to disjoint sets laid out by the given condition, and this 27 number of assignments corresponds to each distinct pair of (X, Y).

11. (A)

First, let's assign three elements to $|Y \cap X^c|$ by $\binom{5}{3}$. Suppose $\{a, b, c\} = Y \cap X^c$. Then, there are two remaining elements that can be assigned either to $Y \cap X$, $X \cap Y^c$, or $(X \cup Y)^c$. Hence, there are
$$\binom{5}{3} \times 3^2 = 90$$
ways to assign each element in proper positions, whose number corresponds to the number of distinct pairs of (X, Y).

12. (C)

This problem looked like a permutation allowing repetition, but the given condition somehow prevents it from being solved by this concept. So, we perform partition of natural numbers to find out all possible number of cases, i.e.,

$$a + b + c = 5$$
$$3 + 1 + 1 = 5$$
$$2 + 2 + 1 = 5$$

Now, we partition five distinct marbles into these groups, by

$$\binom{5}{3} \times \binom{2}{1} \times \binom{1}{1} \times \frac{1}{2!} + \binom{5}{2} \times \binom{3}{2} \times \binom{1}{1} \times \frac{1}{2!}$$

Lastly, we must distribute these marbles into three different boxes by

$$\binom{5}{3} \times \binom{2}{1} \times \binom{1}{1} \times \frac{1}{2!} \times 3! + \binom{5}{2} \times \binom{3}{2} \times \binom{1}{1} \times \frac{1}{2!} \times 3! = 60 + 90 = 150$$

different number of ways.

13. (B)

This problem is a typical combination allowing repetition, also known as circles and bars. Let a, b, and c be the number of marbles in each distinct box. Then, $a + b + c = 5$ where $a, b, c \geq 0$. According to the partition of whole numbers, we get

$$a + b + c = 5$$
$$5 + 0 + 0 = 5$$
$$4 + 1 + 0 = 5$$
$$3 + 2 + 0 = 5$$
$$3 + 1 + 1 = 5$$
$$2 + 2 + 1 = 5$$

Since the boxes are distinct, we must rearrange the given triples. First, $(5, 0, 0)$ has $\binom{3}{1}$ number of rearrangements. Second, $(4, 1, 0)$ has $3!$ number of rearrangements. Third, $(3, 2, 0)$ has $3!$ number of rearrangements. Fourth, $(3, 1, 1)$ has $\binom{3}{1}$ number of rearrangements. Fifth, $(2, 2, 1)$ has $\binom{3}{1}$ number of rearrangements. Hence, there are $3 + 6 + 6 + 3 + 3 = 21$ number of arrangements of 5 indistinct marbles into 3 distinguishable boxes. On the other hand, there exists one-to-one correspondence between the number of arrangements and the configuration of 5 circles and 2 bars, i.e., $\binom{7}{2} = 21$.

14. (D)

Let a, b, and c be the number of marbles in each distinct box. Then, $a+b+c=5$ where $a,b,c \geq 1$. According to the partition of whole numbers satisfying the given condition, we get

$$a+b+c=5$$
$$3+1+1=5$$
$$2+2+1=5$$

There are $\binom{3}{1}$ number of arranging $(3,1,1)$, and $\binom{3}{1}$ number of arranging $(2,2,1)$. Hence, there are 6 ways to place 5 indistinct marbles into 3 distinct boxes.

We can try solving this problem using one-to-one correspondence and circles and bars. First, let $a = a'+1$, $b = b'+1$ and $c = c'+1$ where $a', b', c' \geq 0$. Then, $a+b+c=5$ implies that $a'+b'+c'=2$. There are 2 circles and 2 bars in this question. Have a look at the following one-to-one correspondence to understand why this is called "circles and bars."

$$a'+b'+c'=2$$
$$2+0+0=2$$
$$0+2+0=2$$
$$0+0+2=2$$
$$1+1+0=2$$
$$1+0+1=2$$
$$0+1+1=2$$

All of these six configurations match perfectly with the configurations using $\bigcirc, \bigcirc, |, |$. The following nicely shows it.

$$a'+b'+c'=2$$
$$2+0+0 = \bigcirc, \bigcirc, |, |$$
$$0+2+0 = |, \bigcirc, \bigcirc, |$$
$$0+0+2 = |, |, \bigcirc, \bigcirc$$
$$1+1+0 = \bigcirc, |, \bigcirc, |$$
$$1+0+1 = \bigcirc, |, |, \bigcirc$$
$$0+1+1 = |, \bigcirc, |, \bigcirc$$

15. (A)

There are two ways of solving this problem. First, we can perform casework. In particular, if $1 \leq a \leq b \leq c \leq 4$, then we can case-enumerate in four subcases.

- $a < b < c$: Out of 4 numbers, we choose 3 numbers, so there are $\binom{4}{3} = 4$ ways to choose (a, b, c) satisfying $a < b < c$.

- $a = b < c$: Out of 4 numbers, we choose 2 numbers, so there are $\binom{4}{2} = 6$ ways to choose (a, b, c) satisfying $a = b < c$.

- $a < b = c$: Out of 4 numbers, we choose 2 numbers, so there are $\binom{4}{2} = 6$ ways to choose (a, b, c) satisfying $a < b = c$.

- $a = b = c$: Out of 4 numbers, we choose 1 number, so there are $\binom{4}{1} = 4$ ways to choose (a, b, c) satisfying $a = b = c$.

Hence, there are 20 ways to choose (a, b, c) satisfying $1 \leq a \leq b \leq c \leq 4$. On the other hand, we can use "circles and bars" to solve this question, using one-to-one correspondence. Let x_1 be the number of 1s in (a, b, c), x_2 be the number of 2s in (a, b, c), x_3 be the number of 3s in (a, b, c) and x_4 be the number of 4s in (a, b, c). Then, $x_1 + x_2 + x_3 + x_4 = 3$. By circles and bars, there are $\binom{6}{3} = 20$ triples of (a, b, c).

16. (C)

This is similar to the previous question. Since $2^1 | 2^a | 2^b | 2^c | 2^5$, we are solving for $1 \leq a \leq b \leq c \leq 5$.

First, let's perform casework.

- $a < b < c$: Out of 5 numbers, we choose 3 numbers, so there are $\binom{5}{3} = 10$ ways to choose (a, b, c) satisfying $a < b < c$.

- $a = b < c$: Out of 5 numbers, we choose 2 numbers, so there are $\binom{5}{2} = 10$ ways to choose (a, b, c) satisfying $a = b < c$.

- $a < b = c$: Out of 5 numbers, we choose 2 numbers, so there are $\binom{5}{2} = 10$ ways to choose (a, b, c) satisfying $a < b = c$.

- $a = b = c$: Out of 5 numberse, we choose 1 number, so there are $\binom{5}{1} = 5$ ways to choose (a, b, c) satisfying $a = b = c$.

Hence, there are 35 ways to choose (a, b, c) satisfying the given condition. On the other hand, using one-to-one correspondence, let x_k be the number of appearances of ks in (a, b, c) where $k = 1, 2, 3, 4, 5$. Then, $\sum_{k=1}^{5} x_k = 3$ implies that there are $\binom{7}{3} = 35$ ways to choose (a, b, c).

17. (B)

There are many ways to solve this problem. The first method is an introduction of a new variable w and solve it as $x + y + z + w = 5$. How does this work? We can find one-to-one correspondence between the number of 4-tuples satisfying $x + y + z + w = 5$ and $x + y + z \leq 5$. If $w = 0$, then we have $x + y + z = 5$, which is equivalent to $x + y + z + 0 = 5$. If $w = 1$, then we have $x + y + z = 4$, equivalent to $x + y + z + 1 = 5$. If $w = 2$, then we have $x + y + z = 3$, equivalent to $x + y + z + 2 = 5$. If $w = 3$, then we have $x + y + z = 2$, equivalent to $x + y + z + 3 = 5$. If $w = 4$, then we have $x + y + z = 1$, equivalent to $x + y + z + 4 = 5$. If $w = 5$, then we have $x + y + z = 0$, equivalent to $x + y + z + 5 = 5$. Hence, using circles and bars, we get $\binom{8}{3}$ number of triples satisfying $x + y + z \leq 5$.

The second method is a hockey-stick identity, i.e.,

$$\binom{n}{2} + \binom{n-1}{2} + \binom{n-2}{2} + \cdots + \binom{2}{2} = \binom{n+1}{3}$$

A short proof of this can be laid out as a "casework." Let's suppose we have a set $\{1, 2, 3, 4, 5, \cdots, n+1\}$. We would like to figure out the number of subsets with three elements. In order to do so, we perform casework on the smallest element. Assume that the smallest element is 1, then we must choose 2 elements out of n elements, i.e., $\binom{n}{2}$. Now, assume that the smallest element is 2, then we must choose 2 elements out of $n - 1$ elements, i.e., $\binom{n-1}{2}$. We keep doing this process until we reach the smallest element as $n - 1$. In this case, we must choose 2 elements out of $\{n, n+1\}$, i.e., $\binom{2}{2}$. Since case enumeration is exhaustive and comprehensive, we conlcude that we found all possible three-element subsets.

18. (B)

Assume a, b, and c are positive. Then, $a = 7^{a'}$, $b = 7^{b'}$ and $c = 7^{c'}$ where a', b', and c' are non-negative integers. Then, $a' + b' + c' = n$ has $\binom{n+2}{2}$ number of solutions. That being written, if a, b, and c are allowed to be negative, the signs of (a, b, c) fall under the following four possibilities - $(+, +, +)$, $(-, -, +)$, $(-, +, -)$, and $(+, -, -)$. Hence,

$$4 \times \binom{n+2}{2} = 312$$
$$\binom{n+2}{2} = 78$$
$$(n+2) \cdot (n+1) = 156$$
$$13 \cdot 12 = 156$$

This implies $n = 11$.

19. (A)

Let $\{a, b, c, d\}$ written in increasing order. This implies that $a = a' + 1$, $b = b' + 3$, $c = c' + 5$ and $d = d' + 7$, where $0 \leq a' \leq b' \leq c' \leq d' \leq 3$. Let x_0 be the number of 0's in (a', b', c', d'), x_1 the number of 1's in (a', b', c', d') and x_2 the number of 2's in (a', b', c', d') and x_3 the number of 3's in (a', b', c', d'). Therefore, we use circles and bars to solve $x_0 + x_1 + x_2 + x_3 = 4$. There are $\binom{7}{3} = 35$ number of (x_0, x_1, x_2, x_3), which has one-to-one correspondence with (a', b', c', d'). Since the conditions $a = a' + 1$, $b = b' + 3$, $c = c' + 5$ and $d = d' + 7$ preserve one-to-one correspondence, we conclude that there are 35 different 4-element subsets.

20. (C)

Let $a = 2a' + 1$, $b = 2b' + 1$ and $c = 2c' + 1$, where $a', b', c' \geq 0$. Then, by circles and bars,

$$a + b + c = 31$$
$$(2a' + 1) + (2b' + 1) + (2c' + 1) = 31$$
$$2a' + 2b' + 2c' = 28$$
$$a' + b' + c' = 14$$

Hence, there are 120 distinct triples of (a', b', c') which has one-to-one correspondence with (a, b, c).

TOPIC 3

Extending to Probability

3.1 Extending to Probability

The probability theory we learn all began with Fermat and Pascal. In this section, there are a few terms with examples to explain what we must know in order to extend all counting methods to compute the probability.

In the language of probability theory, we say the set of all possible results by any experiment or trial[1] as the sample space. Here, the subset of sample space is called "**event**," a set of outcomes of a certain experiment. If an "event" is a singleton set, we call it "elementary event" or "atomic event." In other words,

$$\text{Sample space} = \cup_{i=1}^{n} \{\text{elementary event}_i\}.$$

Example Find the sample space and all elementary events when someone rolls a fair die.

Step-by-step Solution
#1. The sample space is a set of all possible outcomes, $S = \{1, 2, 3, 4, 5, 6\}$.
#2. All elementary events are $\{1\}, \{2\}, \{3\}, \{4\}, \{5\}$ and $\{6\}$, which are also known as **singletons**.

Example Find the sample space and all elementary events when two fair coins are flipped.

Step-by-step Solution
#1. The sample space is a set of all possible outcomes, $S = \{HH, HT, TH, TT\}$.
#2. All elementary events are $\{HH\}, \{HT\}, \{TH\}$, and $\{TT\}$.

As one can notice, the size of the sample size is the number of elementary events. We normally assume that each elementary event occurs with equal likelyhood. If there are r number of elementary events in event A, out of n elementary events in sample space, then the probability that an event A will occur, denoted by $P(A)$, is equal to $\frac{|A|}{|S|} = \frac{r}{n}$ where $0 \leq P(A) \leq 1$. In particular, given an arbitrary event A in sample space S,

- $0 \leq P(A) \leq 1$
- $P(\emptyset) = 0$ and $P(S) = 1$.

where $\emptyset$ is a set with no elementary event, and S is the set of events including all elementary events.

---

[1] In probability theory, an experiment or trial is a procedure that can be infinitely or finitely repeated and has a well-defined set of possible outcomes, known as the sample space.

One of the most important ideas that distinguishes "counting (casework and frequency)" and "probability (chance of occurrence)" is the notion of "elementary event" or "atomic event." The golden rule to remember is that if the sample size is n, then each of the elementary event has equal likelihood of $\frac{1}{n}$, which is drastically different from "counting." In counting, if objects are indistinguishable, we delete the overcounts. In probability, if the elements are indistinguishable, we consider them distinct. For instance, let's suppose we are given with five balls labeled with characters.

If we are interested in finding the probability of choosing a ball labeled with A or the probability of choosing a ball labeled with boldfaced letters, if one of the balls are selected at random, we face a dilemma.

- In terms of distinct characters, we have two types : Ⓐ or Ⓑ. Does this mean that we have the probability of $\frac{1}{2}$ of choosing a ball labeled with A? Or, in terms of thickness of characters, we have two types : the lean type or the bold type. Does this mean we have the probability of $\frac{1}{2}$ for choosing a bold-faced ball? Hmm...

- In fact, according to what we have learned so far, we have answered this question as such. The probability of choosing a ball labeled with A is $\frac{2}{5}$, and that of choosing a ball labeled with boldface is $\frac{3}{5}$.

In other words, even though some of the balls labeled with characters are identical-looking, when we compute probability, we must consider them all distinct, since the elementary events(in this case, singletons) are {Ⓐ}, {**Ⓐ**}, {Ⓑ}, {**Ⓑ**}, and {**Ⓑ**}. There are five distinct elementary events, considering all of identical-looking balls different, each of which is attached with the equal probability of $\frac{1}{5}$. Have a look at the following example.

Example Given a set $\{1, 1, 2, 2\}$, compute the probability of choosing two different numbers if two numbers are selected from the set.

Step-by-step Solution
#1. Find the sample space, i.e., $4 \times 3 = 12$. Let's find out the elementary events. In order to find such, we put each element with indices, i.e., $\{1_x, 1_y, 2_x, 2_y\}$.
#2. We have 12 elementary events: $\{(1_x, 1_y)\}$, $\{(1_x, 2_x)\}$, $\{(1_x, 2_y)\}$, $\{(1_y, 2_x)\}$, $\{(1_y, 2_y)\}$, $\{(2_x, 2_y)\}$, $\{(1_y, 1_x)\}$, $\{(2_x, 1_x)\}$, $\{(2_y, 1_x)\}$, $\{(2_x, 1_y)\}$, $\{(2_y, 1_y)\}$, $\{(2_y, 2_x)\}$.
#3. The probability satisfying the given condition equals $\frac{8}{12} = \frac{2}{3}$.

Is this the only way of computing probabilities? Not really. We may use the rules of addition and multiplication of probability.

The following rules of addition and multiplication of probability may be stated as follows.

- We "add" if there is a phrase "or."

- We "multiply" when two or more events occur in a consecutive manner.

The rule of addition is not so difficult, but the rule of multiplication depends on the following two sub-rules.

- If two events A and B are dependent, then

$$P(A \cap B) = P(A) \times P(B|A) = P(B) \times P(A|B)$$

  where $P(A|B)$ is the probability of an event A to occur when B occurred.

- If two events A and B are independent, then $P(A \cap B) = P(A) \times P(B)$.

So, when do we choose "counting" rules, using combination and permutation, or rules of addition/multiplication of probability?

- Counting method - combination :
  ① Assume that we have a uniform probability distribution for each elementary event.
  ② The denominator is computed by unordered arrangement of objects, i.e., combination.
  ③ The numerator takes in "one" specific order that one likes to use. Do not multiply by the number of orders formed when one switches the order of computation.

- Counting method - permutation :
  ① Assume that we have a uniform probability distribution for each elementary event. ② The denominator is computed by ordered arrangement of objects, i.e., permutation.
  ③ The numerator takes all possible orders.

- Rules of addition/multiplication of probability :
  ① Assume that we have a uniform probability distribution for each elementary event.
  ② Multiply dependent(or independent) probabilities as one likes, since $P(A \cap B) = P(A) \cdot P(B|A) = P(B) \cdot P(A|B)$. (Choose your preferred order of computation.)
  ③ If there are "distinct" kinds included, multiply by the number of orders formed when the order of computation changes.
  ④ If there is no "distinct" kind included, leave it untouched.

This being written, counting methods of using combination or permutation are both limited in a way that a selection with replacement cannot be directly solved using the first two methods. Hence, we must practice solving probability questions utilizing all three methods, though some of the methods might be preferred in certain cases due to the brevity of solution. There are some cases when we use the rule of multiplication of probability. The first canse is when there are conditions on specific places when we arrange objects.

Example If two As and four Bs are arranged in a row, find the probability of when the second A appears in the sixth position, arranged from left to right.

Step-by-step Solution
#1. Look at the last position. When A appears in the sixth time, it means that the last position must be filled with A first.
#2. We get the probability of $\frac{2}{6} = \frac{1}{3}$ to fill the last position with A.
#3. Now, all the other positions have no conditions stated, so we consider the probability of filling other positions as 1.
#4. Hence, $\frac{1}{3} \times 1 = \frac{1}{3}$.

The second case is when we group people into subgroups with specific conditions. Have a look at the following example.

Example If eight people, including Bob and Bo, are divided into four groups of two members each, compute the probability that Bob and Bo will be in the same group.

Step-by-step Solution
#1. Partition eight into $2+2+2+2$ such that

$$(①,②), (③,④), (⑤,⑥), (⑦,⑧)$$

#2. Ask Bob to determine where he wants to go. He can choose any number with the probability of $\frac{8}{8}$.
#3. As soon as Bob chooses his number, then Bo can only choose one place with the probability of $\frac{1}{7}$. Without loss of generality, if Bob chooses 1, then Bo must choose 2.
#4. Hence, the probability that Bob and Bo will be placed in the same group is $\frac{1}{7}$.

On the other hand, we could have solved the question above, using counting method as well, which directly uses partition of sets, i.e.,

$$\frac{\frac{\binom{6}{2} \cdot \binom{4}{2} \cdot \binom{2}{2}}{3!}}{\frac{\binom{8}{2} \cdot \binom{6}{2} \cdot \binom{4}{2} \cdot \binom{2}{2}}{4!}} = \frac{1}{7}$$

3.2 Conditional Probability

Out of two events A and B of a sample space S, we denote the conditional probability of A given that B occurred as $P(A|B)$, which is computed by

$$P(A|B) = \frac{P(A \cap B)}{P(B)} = \frac{n(A \cap B)/n(S)}{n(B)/n(S)} = \frac{n(A \cap B)}{n(B)}$$

which shows that the size of the denominator is shrunk down to $n(B)$, whose Venn diagram parts can be illustrated by the following figure.

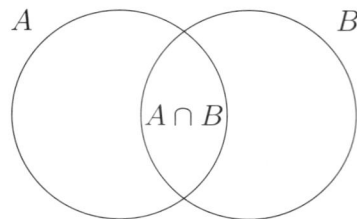

The definition of conditional probability brings forth two identities.

- $P(A \cap B) = P(B) \cdot P(A|B) = P(A) \cdot P(B|A)$.
- $P(A^c|B) + P(A|B) = 1$.

Example Assume there are ten students at Math School, participating in extracurricular activities such that three students are doing math competition, three students are doing computer science, and four students are doing math modeling. Assuming that a student participates in at least one activity, and there is no student participating in at least two activities at the same time, compute the probability of selecting two students who are doing math competition or math modeling, if two selected students out of ten students are in the same group.

Step-by-step Solution
#1. Let event A be the set of unordered pair of students doing math competition or math modeling. Let event B the set of of undered pair of students in the same group.
#2. Then, $|B| = \binom{3}{2} + \binom{3}{2} + \binom{4}{2} = 12$.
#3. Then, $|A \cap B| = \binom{3}{2} + \binom{4}{2} = 9$.
#4. Hence, $P(A|B) = \frac{9}{12} = \frac{3}{4}$.

In other words, if we partition 10 into three groups satisfying the condition, we get $(1,2), (1,3), (2,3), (4,5), (4,6), (5,6), (7,8), (7,9), (7,10), (8,9), (8,10), (9,10)$ as a shrunk sample space. Out of these 12 elements, we simply choose $(1,2), (1,3), (2,3), (7,8), (7,9), (7,10), (8,9), (8,10), (9,10)$.

3.3 Geometric Probability

In its most elementary form, geometric probability is dealt in school work, in terms of a single-variable approach. However, if there are are more variables to cover, we should extend the idea of "proportion."

- Single variable : length proportion.
- Two variables : area proportion.
- Three variables : volume proportion, or conditional probability in two variables.

Example If a real number x is chosen at random from $[0, 1]$, compute the probability that $\frac{1}{2} \leq x \leq 1$.

Step-by-step Solution
#1. The sample space is $[0, 1]$, so its length is 1.
#2. The event size is $1/2$, which is the length of $[1/2, 1]$.
#3. Since there is only one variable, we use the length ratio to compute the probability, i.e., $\frac{1/2}{1} = \frac{1}{2}$.

Example If real numbers x and y are chosen at random from $[0, 1]$, compute the probability that $|x - y| \leq \frac{1}{2}$.

Step-by-step Solution
#1. Let $x \in [0, 1]$ and $y \in [0, 1]$.
#2. Since $|x - y| \leq \frac{1}{2}$, we get $x - \frac{1}{2} \leq y \leq x + \frac{1}{2}$.
#3. Look at the following figure, showing the conditions stated in the problem.

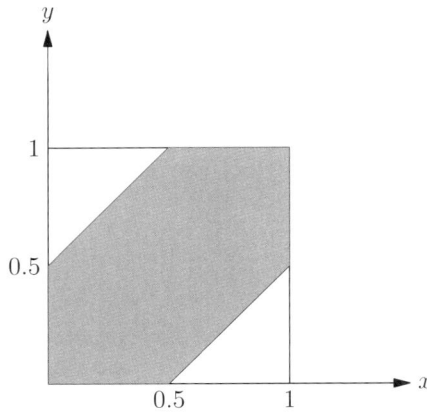

The probability we look for equals the ratio of the area of hexagon to that of square, which is $\frac{6}{8} = \frac{3}{4}$.

Practice

1. Given a set of numbers $\{1, 1, 2, 2, 3, 3, 4\}$, compute the probability of selecting two cards whose sum is prime, assuming there is no replacement of cards

(A) $\dfrac{11}{21}$ (B) $\dfrac{13}{21}$ (C) $\dfrac{14}{21}$ (D) $\dfrac{5}{7}$ (E) $\dfrac{16}{21}$

2. If 11 letters that consist of a word "MISSISSIPPI" are rearranged in a row, compute the probability that all Ps are adjacent to one another.

(A) $\dfrac{2}{11}$ (B) $\dfrac{3}{11}$ (C) $\dfrac{4}{11}$ (D) $\dfrac{5}{11}$ (E) $\dfrac{6}{11}$

3. Given a set of letters $\{A, B, B, C, D, E, F\}$, if all seven letters are arranged in a row, compute the probability that C is always right-side of Bs.

(A) $\dfrac{1}{2}$ (B) $\dfrac{1}{3}$ (C) $\dfrac{1}{4}$ (D) $\dfrac{1}{5}$ (E) $\dfrac{1}{6}$

4. Given a set of numbers $\{1, 1, 2, 2, 2, 3, 4\}$, if all 7 numbers are arranged in a row, compute the probability that 2 is in its front and end.

(A) $\dfrac{1}{7}$ (B) $\dfrac{2}{7}$ (C) $\dfrac{3}{7}$ (D) $\dfrac{4}{7}$ (E) $\dfrac{5}{7}$

5. If ten people, Bob and Bo, are grouped into three small groups with 5, 3, and 2 members each, compute the probability that Bob and Bo are in the same group.

(A) $\dfrac{5}{18}$ (B) $\dfrac{13}{45}$ (C) $\dfrac{3}{10}$ (D) $\dfrac{14}{45}$ (E) $\dfrac{1}{3}$

6. A bag contains two red beads and four green beads. If Bob pulls out one bead per day, what is the probability that he pulls out red bead(s) in the first day <u>or</u> the last day?

(A) $\dfrac{8}{15}$ (B) $\dfrac{17}{30}$ (C) $\dfrac{3}{5}$ (D) $\dfrac{19}{30}$ (E) $\dfrac{2}{3}$

7. If five people, including Bob and Bo, are to be seated in a row of chairs, Bob and Bo secretly chose their favorite seats, not the same seats, in minds. Compute the probability of Bob and Bo not sitting in their original seats in mind.

(A) $\dfrac{11}{20}$ 　　(B) $\dfrac{13}{20}$ 　　(C) $\dfrac{3}{4}$ 　　(D) $\dfrac{17}{20}$ 　　(E) $\dfrac{19}{20}$

8. Bo flips over the cards of a standard 52-card deck one at a time. What is the probability that he flips over the ace of clubs before any face card (jack, queen or king)?

(A) $\dfrac{1}{13}$ 　　(B) $\dfrac{1}{12}$ 　　(C) $\dfrac{1}{11}$ 　　(D) $\dfrac{1}{10}$ 　　(E) $\dfrac{1}{9}$

9. A drawer contains 3 white beads and 6 black beads. Nine beads are drawn out of the box one at a time. What is the probability the last two beads drawn out have different colors?

(A) $\dfrac{7}{10}$ (B) $\dfrac{2}{3}$ (C) $\dfrac{5}{7}$ (D) $\dfrac{3}{4}$ (E) $\dfrac{1}{2}$

10. If eight people, four males and four females, are to be teamed up in four pairs, compute the probability when there are only two teams of mixed gender.

(A) $\dfrac{18}{35}$ (B) $\dfrac{24}{35}$ (C) $\dfrac{5}{7}$ (D) $\dfrac{26}{35}$ (E) $\dfrac{27}{35}$

11. If Bob and Bo play a tennis match with such rule that a player who wins two consecutive rounds in a row or wins three rounds first wins the tennis match, compute the probability that Bob wins the match, given that he has won the first round.

(A) $\dfrac{9}{16}$ (B) $\dfrac{11}{16}$ (C) $\dfrac{13}{16}$ (D) $\dfrac{15}{16}$ (E) $\dfrac{31}{32}$

12. Imagine there are two identical-looking bags such that the first bag contains four red beads and six green beads, and the second bag contains two red beads and eight green beads. If a bag is chosen at random and a bead is selected at random, find the probability that a bead was originally from the first bag, given that the bead is red.

(A) $\dfrac{1}{4}$ (B) $\dfrac{2}{3}$ (C) $\dfrac{1}{2}$ (D) $\dfrac{3}{4}$ (E) $\dfrac{4}{5}$

13. One blue bead, one yellow bead, and two green beads are placed in a bag. If two beads are chosen at random, compute the probability of choosing two green beads, given that one of the beads is green.

(A) $\dfrac{1}{3}$ (B) $\dfrac{1}{4}$ (C) $\dfrac{1}{5}$ (D) $\dfrac{1}{6}$ (E) $\dfrac{1}{7}$

14. Bob and Bo draw a straw from a set of six straws with different lengths, allowing replacement. If Bob and Bo select straws with equal lengths, then they flip a fair coin twice. Otherwise, they flip a fair coin four times. If the number of heads equals that of tails, compute the probability that the coin is tossed twice.

(A) $\dfrac{3}{19}$ (B) $\dfrac{4}{19}$ (C) $\dfrac{5}{19}$ (D) $\dfrac{6}{19}$ (E) $\dfrac{7}{19}$

15. Bob and Bo each arrive at a museum at a random time between 3:00 and 4:00. If Bob arrives after Bo, what is the probability that Bo arrived before 3:30?

(A) $\dfrac{1}{4}$ (B) $\dfrac{3}{4}$ (C) $\dfrac{1}{2}$ (D) $\dfrac{3}{8}$ (E) $\dfrac{5}{8}$

16. Given two real numbers x and y such that $x, y \in [0, 1]$, compute the probability that x, y and 1 form a triangle, given that $y \leq x$.

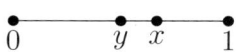

(A) $\dfrac{1}{4}$ (B) $\dfrac{3}{4}$ (C) $\dfrac{1}{2}$ (D) $\dfrac{3}{8}$ (E) $\dfrac{5}{8}$

17. Two numbers between 0 and 1 on a number line, x and y, are to be chosen at random. What is the probability that the second number, y, chosen will exceed the first number chosen, x, by a distance greater than $\frac{1}{3}$ unit on the number line?

(A) $\frac{1}{9}$ (B) $\frac{2}{9}$ (C) $\frac{1}{3}$ (D) $\frac{4}{9}$ (E) $\frac{5}{9}$

18. Bob needs to catch a flight. The airplane arrives at the terminal randomly some time between 2:00 and 3:00, has its passengers seated for 10 minutes, and then leaves. If Bob arrives randomly between 2:00 and 3:00, what is the probability that the airplane will be there when Bob reaches the terminal?

(A) $\frac{1}{4}$ (B) $\frac{5}{18}$ (C) $\frac{11}{36}$ (D) $\frac{13}{36}$ (E) $\frac{11}{72}$

19. Given a set of points satisfying $x^2 + y^2 = 1$, let A and B be two points on the circle chosen randomly and independently. Find the probability the pairwise distance between A and B is at most 1.

(A) $\dfrac{1}{2}$ (B) $\dfrac{1}{3}$ (C) $\dfrac{2}{5}$ (D) $\dfrac{3}{7}$ (E) $\dfrac{4}{7}$

20. Given three real numbers x, y, and z such that $0 \leq x \leq 2$, $0 \leq y \leq 2$ and $0 \leq z \leq 2$, compute the probability that $x - y \leq 1$, if $x < z$ and $y < z$.

(A) $\dfrac{3}{13}$ (B) $\dfrac{5}{16}$ (C) $\dfrac{7}{24}$ (D) $\dfrac{9}{26}$ (E) $\dfrac{11}{30}$

Solution

1. (B)

We are dealing with probability, so we can safely assume that the given set of numbers can be considered as $\{1_a, 1_b, 2_a, 2_b, 3_a, 3_b, 4\}$. The total sample space consists of all pairs (a, b) such that a and b are elements of the set above, which can be counted upto 21 distinct pairs. Now, list all the pairs that satisfy the given condition, i.e.

$$(a, b) = (1, 1)$$
$$= (1, 2)$$
$$= (2, 1)$$
$$= (2, 3)$$
$$= (3, 2)$$
$$= (1, 4)$$
$$= (4, 1)$$
$$= (3, 4)$$
$$= (4, 3)$$

Now, for $(1, 1)$, there are 2 distinguishable cases, i.e., $(1_a, 1_b)$ and $(1_b, 1_a)$. For $(1, 2)$ there are 4 distinguishable cases, i.e., $(1_a, 2_a)$, $(1_b, 2_a)$, $(1_a, 2_b)$, and $(1_b, 2_b)$. For $(2, 1)$, there are 4 distinguishable cases, i.e., $(2_a, 1_a)$, $(2_a, 1_b)$, $(2_b, 1_a)$ and $(2_b, 1_b)$. For $(2, 3)$ and $(3, 2)$, there are 8 possible cases, i.e., $(2_a, 3_a)$, $(2_a, 3_b)$, $\cdots$, $(3_b, 2_a)$, and $(3_b, 2_b)$. Likewise, for $(1, 4)$ and $(4, 1)$, there are 4 distinguishable cases, i.e., $(1_a, 4)$, $(1_b, 4)$, $(4, 1_a)$, and $(4, 1_b)$. Lastly, for $(3, 4)$ and $(4, 3)$, there are 4 distinguishable cases, i.e., $(3_a, 4)$, $(3_b, 4)$ $(4, 3_a)$ and $(4, 3_b)$. Hence, there are 26 pairs out of 42 pairs. Hence, the answer is $\frac{13}{21}$.

2. (A)

Solution 1

This is a probability question. So, consider $\{M, I, S, S, I, S, S, I, P, P, I\}$ as $\{M, I_1, S_1, S_2, I_2, S_3, S_4, I_3, P_1, P_2, I_4\}$. Hence, out of permutations with 11 different letters, we simply count the number of cases when P_1 and P_2 are adjacent to each other. Therefore, we consider P_1 and P_2 into a single bundle, arrange ten objects, then multiply by 2 to count for the order of arrangements between P_1 and P_2, i.e., the rearrangement of $(P_1, P_2), M, I_1, I_2, I_3, I_4, S_1, S_2, S_3, S_4$ where $(P_1, P_2) \neq (P_2, P_1)$. Hence, the probability of two Ps adjacent to each other is

$$\frac{10! \times 2!}{11!} = \frac{2}{11}$$

Solution 2

Given eleven spots to fill, i.e, ①②③⋯⑪, we can perform caseworks in the following manners. If P_1 goes in ① with the probability of $\frac{1}{11}$, then P_2 should go into ② with the probability of $\frac{1}{10}$. Likewise, if P_1 goes in ② with the probability of $\frac{1}{11}$, then P_2 should go in either ① or ③ with the probability of $\frac{2}{10}$. Perform all the caseworks until P_1 goes in ⑪ with the probability of $\frac{1}{11}$. Taking the sum of all probability cases, we get

$$\frac{1}{11} \times \frac{1}{10} + \frac{1}{11} \times \frac{2}{11} + \cdots + \frac{1}{11} \times \frac{2}{10} + \frac{1}{11} \times \frac{1}{10} = \frac{20}{110} = \frac{2}{11}$$

3. (B)

Solution 1

Let's solve it using permutation. The probability that C is always right-side of Bs can be written as

$$\frac{\frac{7!}{3!} \times 2!}{7!} = \frac{1}{3}$$

Solution 2

This deals with relative positions of C and Bs. Since we deal with probability, we consider all Bs distinct, so name them as B_1 and B_2. Hence, we are permuting C, B_1 and B_2 to get $3!$ number of possible arrangements. Since C must be right-side of Bs, we only get two possible arrangements satisfying the condition, i.e., B_1, B_2, C or B_2, B_1, C.

4. (A)

Solution 1

Let's solve it using permutation. The probability that 2 is in its front and end can be computed as

$$\frac{\frac{5!}{2!}}{\frac{7!}{2!3!}} = \frac{1}{7}$$

Solution 2

Name each position of the seven spots as ①②③④⑤⑥⑦. Now, using the rules of multiplication of probability, placing 2s in ① and ⑦ has the probability of $\frac{3}{7} \times \frac{2}{6} = \frac{1}{7}$.

5. (D)

Solution 1

Use partition of sets to solve this question. The probability that Bob and Bo will be in the same group can be computed as

$$\frac{\binom{8}{3} \cdot \binom{5}{3} \cdot \binom{2}{2} + \binom{8}{5} \cdot \binom{3}{1} \cdot \binom{2}{2} + \binom{8}{5} \cdot \binom{3}{3}}{\binom{10}{5} \cdot \binom{5}{3} \cdot \binom{2}{2}} = \frac{14}{45}$$

Solution 2

Name each position of partitions such as $((01)(02)(03)(04)(05))((06)(07)(08))((09)(10))$. Hence, the probability that Bob and Bo are placed in the same group can be computed as

$$\frac{5}{10} \times \frac{4}{9} + \frac{3}{10} \times \frac{2}{9} + \frac{2}{10} \times \frac{1}{9} = \frac{28}{90} = \frac{14}{45}$$

6. (C)

Solution 1

Use basic combinatorial tools to find out the probability. If the first day is red, then the other days may be permuted using one red and four green beads. Hence, there are $\binom{5}{1} = 5$ ways to permute these beads fixing the first day. On the other hand, if the last day is red, then the other days may be permuted using the equal logic as in the previous case. Hence, there are $\binom{5}{1} = 5$ ways to permute these beads. However, there is one case that is overcounted by both caseworks, i.e, the case when Bob pulls out red beads in both the first day and the last day. Hence, there are 9 possible arrangements satisfying the given condition. The total number of arrangements must be $\binom{6}{2} = 15$, so the probability we want is $\frac{9}{15} = \frac{3}{5}$.

Solution 2

Name the color of the beads selected each day as numbers such as $(1)(2)(3)(4)(5)(6)$. Now, the probability that Bob pulls out red bead(s) in the first day or the last day equals

$$\frac{2}{6} \times \frac{4}{5} + \frac{4}{6} \times \frac{2}{5} + \frac{2}{6} \times \frac{1}{5} = \frac{18}{30} = \frac{3}{5}$$

7. (B)

Solution 1

Assume that Bob is already seated in his favorite seat. Then, there are 4! ways to permute other people into different seats. Likewise, assume that Bo is already seated in his favorite seat. Then, there are 4! ways to permute other people into different seats. There are overcounts when Bob and Bo both sat down in their favorite seats, so get rid of 3!. Hence, the probability we want is

$$1 - \frac{4! + 4! - 3!}{5!} = 1 - \frac{42}{120} = \frac{78}{120} = \frac{13}{20}$$

Solution 2

Label seats as $(1)(2)(3)(4)(5)$. Without loss of generality, assume that Bob's favorite seat is (1) and Bo's favorite seat is (2). Then, we get

$$1 - (\frac{1}{5} + \frac{1}{5} - \frac{1}{5} \times \frac{1}{4}) = 1 - \frac{7}{20} = \frac{13}{20}$$

8. (A)

Solution 1

Using permutation method, the probability we want to

$$\frac{\frac{52!}{13!} \times 12!}{52!} = \frac{1}{13}$$

where 52!/13! indicates that we consider a package containing the ace of clubs and all face cards as one and multiply by the number of arrangements between face cards since the ace of club stays in the front of the package.

Solution 2

We only consider the relative relationship between the ace of clus and face card. Hence, label thirteen positions as ⓪①⓪②⋯⑬. The probability that the ace of clubs goes inside ⓪① is $\frac{1}{13}$.

9. (E)

Solution 1

We must have two beads in the last two draws as either white/black or black/white. This means that the other beads must be pulled out beforehand in $\frac{7!}{2!5!} = 21$ ways. Hence, the probability we want to compute is

$$\frac{21 \times 2}{\binom{9}{3}} = \frac{1}{2}$$

Solution 2

Label each draw with the numbers, i.e., ①②⋯⑧⑨. Now, we easily compute the probability as

$$\frac{3}{9} \times \frac{6}{8} + \frac{6}{9} \times \frac{3}{8} = \frac{36}{72} = \frac{1}{2}$$

10. (B)

Solution 1

Using permutation method, we get the probability as

$$\frac{\frac{4 \times 4 \times 3 \times 3}{2!} \times \binom{2}{2} \times \binom{2}{2}}{\frac{\binom{8}{2}\binom{6}{2}\binom{4}{2}\binom{2}{2}}{4!}} = \frac{24}{35}$$

Solution 2

Label each four groups having two spots each as (①②)(③④)(⑤⑥)(⑦⑧). Then, all we need to do is to send four men in proper positions, i.e.,

$$\binom{4}{2} \times \frac{8}{8} \times \frac{6}{7} \times \frac{4}{6} \times \frac{1}{5} = \frac{24}{35}$$

11. (B)

We must compute the number of cases when Bob wins the first round.

- $P(WW) : \dfrac{1}{4}$.

- $P(WLWW) : \dfrac{1}{16}$

- $P(WLWLW) : \dfrac{1}{32}$

- $P(WLL) : \dfrac{1}{8}$

- $P(WLWLL) : \dfrac{1}{32}$

Hence, out of these probabilities, we only count when Bob wins the match as well. In particular, we get
$$\frac{1/4 + 1/16 + 1/32}{1/4 + 1/16 + 1/32 + 1/8 + 1/32} = \frac{11}{16}$$

12. (B)

$$\begin{aligned}
P(\text{Bag 1}|\text{Red}) &= \frac{P(\text{Bag 1} \cap \text{Red})}{P(\text{Red})} \\
&= \frac{P(\text{Bag 1}) \cdot P(\text{Red}|\text{Bag 1})}{P(\text{Bag 1}) \cdot P(\text{Red}|\text{Bag 1}) + P(\text{Bag 2}) \cdot P(\text{Red}|\text{Bag 2})} \\
&= \frac{\frac{1}{2} \times \frac{4}{10}}{\frac{1}{2} \times \frac{4}{10} + \frac{1}{2} \times \frac{2}{10}} \\
&= \frac{2}{3}
\end{aligned}$$

13. (C)

First, beads can be labeled as B, Y, G_1, and G_2. Now, conditional probability implies that the sample space is shrunk down to $\{BY, BG_1, BG_2, YG_1, YG_2, G_1G_2\}$. Hence,
$$\frac{|\{G_1G_2\}|}{|\{BG_1, BG_2, YG_1, YG_2, G_1G_2\}|} = \frac{1}{5}$$

14. (B)

$$\begin{aligned}
P(\text{equal}|H = T) &= \frac{P(\text{equal} \cap H = T)}{P(H = T)} \\
&= \frac{P(\text{equal}) \cdot P(H = T|\text{ equal })}{P(\text{equal}) \cdot P(H = T|\text{ equal }) + P(\text{different}) \cdot P(H = T|\text{ different })} \\
&= \frac{1/12}{1/12 + 5/16} \\
&= \frac{4}{19}
\end{aligned}$$

15. (B)

This is another conditional probability question mixed with geometric probability. The probability that Bob arrives after Bo is $\frac{1}{2}$. The probability that Bo arrived before $3:30$ and Bob arrives after Bo is $\frac{3}{8}$. Hence, the conditional probability must be $\frac{3/8}{1/2} = \frac{3}{4}$.

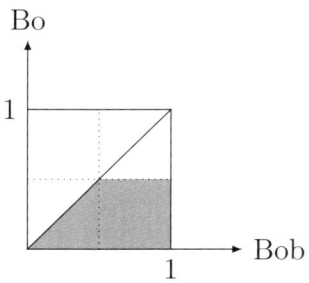

16. (C)

Due to the given constraints, notice that $y \leq x \leq 1$ is the only side length condition that satisfies the original condition. Hence, $1 < y + x$ implies that $y > -x + 1$. We are computing the probability that x, y and 1 form a triangle, given that $y \leq x$, so $\frac{1/4}{1/2} = \frac{1}{2}$.

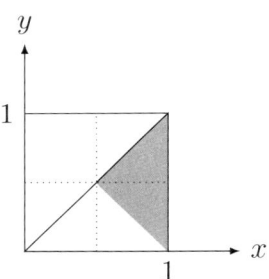

17. (B)

Given the constraints $0 \leq x \leq 1$ and $0 \leq y \leq 1$, we must satisfy $y > x + \frac{1}{3}$. Hence, out of 1×1 square, we are looking for the area proportion of a triangle whose side lengths are $\frac{2}{3}$ and $\frac{2}{3}$, as shown in the figure below. Hence, the probability we want is $\frac{2}{9}$.

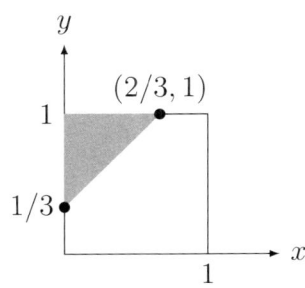

18. (E)

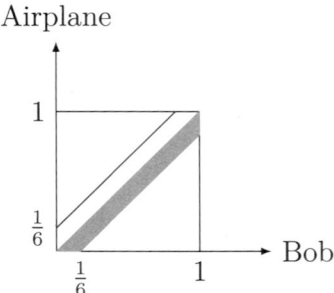

As one can see from the figure above, we are looking for the area proportion of colored region to the unit square. Since airplane must arrive before Bob, we set "airplane<Bob." Likewise, |airplane − Bob| < $\frac{1}{6}$ implies that Bob will not miss the flight. The colored region is half the size of hexagonal strip whose area equals $\frac{11}{36}$, so the probability we want must be $\frac{11}{72}$.

19. (B)

Choose A on the unit circle with the probability of $2\pi/2\pi = 1$. Now, choose B on the unit circle, knowing that A is on the unit circle already. Then, B must be with respect to A in the range of measures of central angle between $-60°$ and $60°$. Hence, the probability of B given A is $1/3$. Since $P(B|A) = P(B)$ by assumption, $P(A \cap B) = P(A) \times P(B) = \frac{1}{3}$.

20. (B)

First, $0 \leq x \leq 2$, $0 \leq y \leq 2$, and $0 \leq z \leq 2$, which gives the volume of 8 units. Since $x < z$ and $y < z$, we get a pyramid of volume $8/3$. Now, since $x - y \leq 1$, then we must subtract smaller pyramid of volume $1 \times 1 \times 1/2 \times 1 \times 1/3 = 1/6$. Therefore, the probability that we want is
$$\frac{8/3 - 1/6}{8} = \frac{5}{16}$$

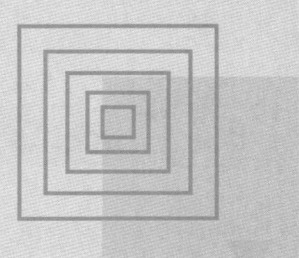

TOPIC 4

Special Themes

4.1 Recurrence Relation

Recurrence relation is a useful tool for counting, a concept of which appears oftentimes in AIME for a long period of time. Recurrence relation always looks at the relationship between some consecutive terms to find out the total values. Normally, questions in AIME or AMC ask the value of nth term usually for n between 10 and 20. The golden rule to solve recurrence equation is to set up proper equations, if necessary, including multiple layers of equations, and find proper base cases to substitute correct values into the equation.

Example (Towers of Hanoi) Assume there are three rods from left to right, and n number of disks of distinct diameters, which can slide onto any rod. There are n number of disks already stacked on one rod in strictly decreasing order. Compute the smallest number of moves required to move 10 stacks to the a designated rod, usually the last rod, following the three rules.

- At one move, you can move one disk at a time.

- Each move consists of taking the upper disk from one of the stacks and placing it on top of another stack or empty rod.

- No disk can be placed on top of a smaller-sized disk.

Step-by-step Solution
#1. We must set up proper relation for nth term. Let x_n be the smallest number of steps required to move n number of stacks from one rod to another.
#2. Then, move the first $n-1$ disks to the second rod in x_{n-1} steps, and move the last disk to the designated rod.
#3. Then, perform another x_{n-1} steps to move the $n-1$ disks in the second rod.
#4. According to what we have observed, $x_n = 2x_{n-1} + 1$.
#5. If $n = 1$, then $x_1 = 1$.
#6. If $n = 2$, then $x_2 = 2x_1 + 1 = 3$. In particular, label disks as ①, ②. At the first step, move ① into the second rod. At the second step, move ② into the designated rod. Then, at the third step, move ① into the designated rod as well.
#7. Now, $x_3 = 2x_2 + 1 = 7$, $x_4 = 2x_3 + 1 = 15$, $x_5 = 2x_4 + 1 = 31$, $x_6 = 2x_5 + 1 = 63$, $x_7 = 2x_6 + 1 = 127$, $x_8 = 2x_7 + 1 = 255$, $x_9 = 2x_8 + 1 = 511$, and $x_{10} = 2x_9 + 1 = 1023$.
#8. Conclude that there are 1023 steps minimally required to move all 10 disks from the first rod to the third rod satisfying the given conditions.
#9. In fact, one can find the closed form of Towers of Hanoi as $x_n = 2^n - 1$.

4.2 Burnside's Lemma

Burnside's lemma appears in group theory counts objects involving symmetry such as rotation or reflection, and such symmetric objects are not to be counted as distinct. It simply counts the number of "orbits" of a finite set acted on a finite group. Here is the lemma. Let G be a finite group that acts on the set X. Let X/G be the set of orbits of X. For any element $g \in G$, then X^g be the set of points of X fixed by g. Then

$$|X/G| = \frac{\sum_{g \in G} |X^g|}{|G|}$$

The above horrible looking notational bashing can be translated into something we know. The lemma simply counts the average number of "symmetrical figures" over all possible symmetries. That being written, let's go over some examples so that we can use the lemma in the competition.

Example Compute the number of different coloring of a 2×2 figure using two colors - blue and green. For instance, the following figure could be one such example.

B	G
B	G

Step-by-step Solution

#1. There are eight possible transformations, i.e., identity, rotation by 90°, rotation by 180°, and rotation by 270°, reflection about the vertical line passing through the center, reflection about the horizontal line passing through the center, reflection about the diagonal that goes southeast direction, and reflection about the diagonal that goes northeast direction.

#2. Identity : As shown in the following figure,

1	2
3	4

there are four regions that are not interfered with by this transformation. Color each region with two possible colors, so there are 2^4 number of ways to color this figure. We say, there are 2^4 elements fixed by this transformation.

#3. Rotation by 90° or 270° : As shown in the following figure,

1	1
1	1

there is only one region that matters after this transformation. Color one of the regions labeled as 1 with two possible colors, and all the other regions labeled as 1 will be colored automatically the same color as the first one. Hence, there are 2^1 number of ways to color this figure. We say, there are 2^1 elements fixed by these transformations.

#4. Rotation by 180° : As shown in the following figure,

1	2
2	1

there are two distinct regions after this transformation. Color regions with 1 or 2 using two colors in 2^2 number of ways. In other words, there are 2^2 elements fixed by this tranformation.

#4. Reflection about either vertical or horizontal line : As shown in the following figures,

1	1
2	2

1	2
1	2

there are 2^2 elements fixed by this transformation.

#5. Reflection about the diagonals : As shown in the following figures,

1	3
3	2

3	1
2	3

there are 2^3 elements fixed by this transformation.

#6. Hence, Burnside's lemma states $\frac{2^4+2^1+2^2+2^1+2^2+2^2+2^3+2^3}{8} = 6$.

Example Compute the number of different coloring of edges of a 2×3 rectangle using yellow, green and purple, assuming that rotations and reflections are not considered to be distinct.

Step-by-step Solution

#1. There are only four transformations, i.e., $|G| = 4$ - identity, rotation by 180°, reflection along the vertical line passing through the center, and reflection along the horizontal line passing through the center.

#2. Identity : there are 3^4 elements fixed by this transformation. Hence, there are $3^4 = 81$ ways to color the edges of a rectangle.

#3. Rotation by 180° : there are 3^2 elements fixed by this transformation. There are $3^2 = 9$ ways to color the edges of a rectangle.

#4. Reflection along the vertical line : there are 3^3 elements fixed by this transformation. There are $3^3 = 27$ ways to color the edges of a rectangle.

#5. Reflection along the horizontal line : there are 3^3 elements fixed by this transformation. There are $3^3 = 27$ ways to color the edges of a rectangle.

#6. Now, this gives $\frac{3^4+3^2+3^3+3^3}{4} = 48$ orbits in total.

4.3 Expected Value and Random Walk

Expected value is known as average, but it oftentimes involves tricky conditions so that it is extremely difficult for students to solve using basic definition of expected value. Normally, if we have a fair die, then the expected value of a single roll is 3.5 because we get the sum of equal weights of each face-value, i.e.,

$$\frac{1+2+3+4+5+6}{6} = 3.5$$

On the other hand, if we were to roll two fair dice to get the expected value of the sum of the rolls, then the definition turns into a bit ugly fraction, i.e.

$$\frac{1}{36}(2) + \frac{2}{36}(3) + \frac{3}{36}(4) + \frac{4}{36}(5) + \frac{5}{36}(6) + \frac{6}{36}(7) + \frac{5}{36}(8) + \frac{4}{36}(9) + \cdots + \frac{1}{36}(12) = 7$$

However, due to the property known as "linearity," we could have easily found the answer by computing it as $E(X_1 + X_2) = E(X_1) + E(X_2) = 3.5 + 3.5$, where $E(X_i)$ is the expected value of a single roll of the ith die. The key idea about linearity of expectation is that double-counting is not making any problem in our counts, and we can localize our analysis when solving a math problem. Oftentimes, we may get random walk problem associated to either expected value or probability. Random walk is a problem that there is an end-state, but it does not specify when it will end. In this case, we must set up an equation to find expected value. Have a look at the following example to understand how to solve such problem that there could be an infinite loop unless the end-state is satisfied.

Example Compute the expected number of coin tosses such that we stop tossing a coin until the first head comes up.

Step-by-step Solution
#1. As the question suggests, there is no indication of when this will stop. In fact, we only know that we should stop tossing a coin whenever the first head comes up.
#2. As you try to formulate this problem, you could try using infinite geometric series[1], i.e.

$$E(X) = 1(\frac{1}{2}) + 2(\frac{1}{2})^2 + 3(\frac{1}{2})^3 + \cdots = \sum_{n=1}^{\infty} \frac{n}{2^n} = 2$$

#3. On the other hand, using random-walk method, we could have set the equation as

$$E = \frac{1}{2}(1) + \frac{1}{2}(1 + E)$$

where $E = 2$.

---

[1] In infinite geometric series, $E(X) = 1/p$ where p is the probability of success.

Practice

1. Given ten arrays of lightbulbs from left to right, if two consecutive light bulbs cannot be turned off, as shown in the example with (O) to represent the lightbulb on and (F) the lightbulb off, compute the total number of arrangements of turning the lights on and off.

(A) 34 (B) 89 (C) 128 (D) 144 (E) 230

2. Given nine arrays of lightbulbs from left to right, if *no two consecutive light bulbs* can be both turned on and *no three consecutive light bulbs* can be all turned off, compute the total number of arrangements of turning the lights on and off.

(A) 13 (B) 18 (C) 21 (D) 31 (E) 41

3. In a "special" forest, it could rain for at most two days, but it will not rain for three days in a row. Find the total number of distinct weather conditions for one full week in the forest.

(A) 65   (B) 73   (C) 81   (D) 83   (E) 100

4. There are only three types of weather conditions in Quarezca, the wonderland of dwarves, i.e., "windy", "sunny" and "rainy." Due to the spell under the powerful wizard called Yurafa, all three types of weathers occur every four consecutive days. How many different weather conditions are there for one full week?

(A) 150   (B) 180   (C) 210   (D) 240   (E) 270

5. Bob the baseball batter could make a hit multiple times, but not three hits in a row. In how many different records can he make for ten attempts in a row?
(A) 500 (B) 504 (C) 508 (D) 512 (E) 516

6. Four identical-looking fair die are rolled at a time. Compute the number of sequences of face-values where each of the face values shown in the last three throws is at least large as the face-value in the previous roll.
(A) 122 (B) 123 (C) 124 (D) 125 (E) 126

7. How many ways are there to fill a 1×11 block into blocks of size 1×1 or 1×2?

(A) 89 (B) 100 (C) 121 (D) 125 (E) 144

8. In how many ways can all faces of a cube be colored using all six colors, "yellow," "green," "blue," "red," "purple," and "brown," where all faces are colored with different colors used once? Two colorings are considered equivalent if two cubes can be obtained by rotating the cube.

(A) 24 (B) 30 (C) 90 (D) 120 (E) 720

9. In how many ways can all faces of a cube be colored using at most two colors - blue and green - where two colorings are considered equivalent if two cubes can be obtained by rotating the cube?

(A) 7 (B) 8 (C) 9 (D) 10 (E) 11

10. In how many ways can all faces of a cube be colored only using at most three colors - blue, green, and yellow - where two colorings are considered equivalent if two cubes can be obtained by rotating the cube?

(A) 48 (B) 52 (C) 57 (D) 62 (E) 67

11. In how many ways can a 3 × 3 square with nine 1 × 1 square be colored using at most two colors - blue and yellow - where two colorings are considered equivalent if two squares can be obtained by rotating the square?

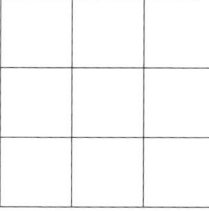

(A) 100 (B) 102 (C) 104 (D) 106 (E) 108

12. In how many ways can a 3 × 3 square with nine 1 × 1 square be colored using six yellows and three greens, where two colorings are considered equivalent if two squares can be obtained by rotating the square?

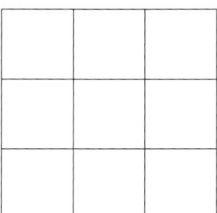

(A) 10 (B) 12 (C) 14 (D) 16 (E) 18

13. Bob rolls a fair six-sided die each morning. If Bob rolls 1, he drinks coffee. If he rolls 2, he drinks milk. If he rolls other numbers, then he rolls again. Assuming that a full month consists of 30 days, what is the expected number of times Bob will roll his die during one full month?
(A) 90 (B) 93 (C) 96 (D) 99 (E) 102

14. Eight cards are arranged around a circle. If two adjacent cards are switched, we call them "relay." If one "relay" is performed, find the average number of cards that are not different from the initial configuration.
(A) 5 (B) 6 (C) 7 (D) 8 (E) 9

15. Out of a 52-card deck, the whole set of cards is shuffled randomly. If the expected number of cards that will be strictly between the ace of spade and ace of heart can be written as m/n in its lowest terms, compute $m+n$.

(A) 49   (B) 51   (C) 52   (D) 53   (E) 54

16. Given a string of 101 numbers, only using 0s, 1s, and 2s, let I be the number of 3-length substrings of all different numbers. For instance, given 01210012, we can compute $I = 3$. Compute the expected value of I with 101 numbers.

(A) 20   (B) 21   (C) 22   (D) 23   (E) 24

17. Given a string of seven numbers around a circle, only using 0s and 1s, let I be the number of 2-length substrings of equal numbers. If the expected number of I can be written as m/n in lowest terms, compute $m + n$.
(A) 8 (B) 9 (C) 10 (D) 11 (E) 12

18. On 5×5 grid of lattice points shown in the figure below, every dot is to be uniformly randomly colored as one of the three colors - yellow, green, or blue. Define "vertex-monochromatic" rectangle if four vertices of a rectangle are monochromatic. If the expected number of vertex-monochromatic rectangles R with vertices chosen from the lattice grids such that the rectangle has one of their parallel sides parrallel to the x-axis and the other sides parallel to the y-axis can be written as m/n where m and n are relatively prime, compute $m + n$.

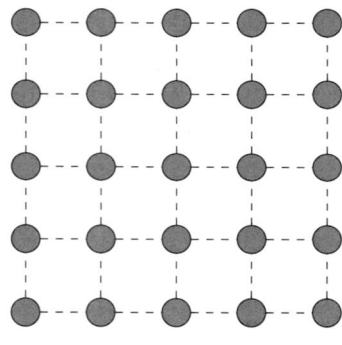

(A) 121 (B) 123 (C) 125 (D) 127 (E) 129

19. An ant starts at one of the non-center dots shown in the figure below and at each step moves along an adjacent edge, with equal probability for any adjacent edge. If this ant continues walking until it gets to the center vertex, compute the product of the expected (average) number of steps required until the first time it gets to the center vertex between that of the steps from four dots along the edges and that of the steps from four dots on the vertices of a large square.

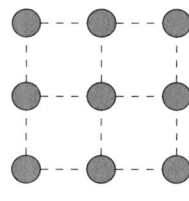

(A) 12   (B) 20   (C) 30   (D) 42   (E) 56

20. An ant is located at a vertex of a 2×2 cube, either at $(0,0,0)$, $(2,0,0)$, $(0,2,0)$, $(0,0,2)$, $(2,2,0)$, $(2,0,2)$, $(0,2,2)$, or $(2,2,2)$. At each step, it moves along the indicated edge to an adjacent point shown in the figure. Compute the expected (average) number of steps for an ant to reach the center of the cube for the first time, if this ant continues walking along the edge at a time until it gets to the destination, where a path already walked can be used again.

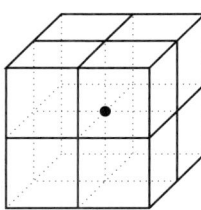

(A) 21   (B) 22   (C) 23   (D) 24   (E) 25

Solution

1. (D)

We begin with finding a proper set of recurrence relations. We first categorize our sequences by looking at the end-states. Let a_n be the number of n-strings that ends with O and b_n be the number of n-strings that ends with F, both of which are satisfying the given conditions. Then,

$$a_n = a_{n-1} + b_{n-1}$$
$$b_n = a_{n-1}$$

Now, a_n must be equal to a_{n-1} added by O in the last spot and b_{n-1} added by O in the last spot. On the other hand, b_n only equals a_{n-1} added by O, since two consecutive Fs cannot occur in our given sequence. Therefore,

$$a_1 = 1, b_1 = 1$$
$$a_2 = 2, b_2 = 1$$
$$a_3 = 3, b_3 = 2$$
$$a_4 = 5, b_4 = 3$$
$$a_5 = 8, b_6 = 5$$
$$a_6 = 13, b_6 = 8$$
$$a_7 = 21, b_7 = 13$$
$$a_8 = 34, b_8 = 21$$
$$a_9 = 55, b_9 = 34$$
$$a_{10} = 89, b_{10} = 55$$

Hence, $a_{10} + b_{10} = 144$.

On the other hand, let the number of "on" be x and let the number of "off" be y. Then, $x + y = 10$ implies that $(x, y) = (10, 0), (9, 1), (8, 2), (7, 3), (6, 4), (5, 5)$. If there are 10 Os and 0 Fs, then everything is okay. We can continue setting up in this form until we reach $(x, y) = (4, 6)$. In particular, we may get two Fs always adajcent to each other in some positions, i.e.,

$$\text{F F O F O F O F O F}$$

In this case, there are at least two consecutive pairs of Fs. Hence, we get

$$\binom{11}{1} + \binom{10}{1} + \binom{9}{2} + \binom{8}{3} + \binom{7}{4} + \binom{6}{5} = 144$$

2. (C)

Let a_n be the number of n-strings that ends with O and b_n be the number of n-strings that ends with F, both of which are satisfying the given conditions. Then,

$$a_n = b_{n-1}$$
$$b_n = a_{n-1} + a_{n-2}$$

Therefore,

$$a_1 = 1, b_1 = 1$$
$$a_2 = 1, b_2 = 2$$
$$a_3 = 2, b_3 = 3$$
$$a_4 = 2, b_4 = 3$$
$$a_5 = 3, b_6 = 4$$
$$a_6 = 4, b_6 = 5$$
$$a_7 = 5, b_7 = 7$$
$$a_8 = 7, b_8 = 9$$
$$a_9 = 9, b_9 = 12$$

Hence, $a_9 + b_9 = 21$.

3. (C)

Let a_n be the number of n-strings that ends with R and b_n be the number of n-strings that ends with N, where R means the day that rains and N means the day that does not rain.

$$a_n = b_{n-1} + b_{n-2}$$
$$b_n = a_{n-1} + b_{n-1}$$

Therefore,

$$a_1 = 1, b_1 = 1$$
$$a_2 = 2, b_2 = 2$$
$$a_3 = 3, b_3 = 4$$
$$a_4 = 6, b_4 = 7$$
$$a_5 = 11, b_6 = 13$$
$$a_6 = 20, b_6 = 24$$
$$a_7 = 37, b_7 = 44$$

Hence, $a_7 + b_7 = 81$. On the other hand, we could have performed casework to compute the number of all cases that match with the given condition. In particular,

- $(R, N) = (0, 7)$ implies that there is only 1 sequence.
- $(R, N) = (1, 6)$ implies that there are 7 sequences.
- $(R, N) = (2, 5)$ implies that there are $\binom{7}{2} = 21$ sequences.
- $(R, N) = (3, 4)$ implies that there are $\binom{5}{3} + 20 = 30$ sequences.
- $(R, N) = (4, 3)$ implies that there are $\binom{4}{4} + \frac{4 \times 3 \times 2}{2!} + \binom{4}{2} = 19$ sequences.
- $(R, N) = (5, 2)$ implies that there are 3 sequences.

Hence, there are $1 + 7 + 21 + 30 + 19 + 3 = 81$ sequences satisfying the given condition.

4. (D)

Let a_n be the number of length-n strings whose repeated letter in the last four consecutive spots appears in the 1st spot. Let b_n be the number of length-n strings whose repeated letter in the last four consecutive spots appears in the 2nd spot. Let c_n be the number of length-n strings whose repeated letter in the last four consecutive spots appear in the 3rd spot. Hence,

$$a_n = a_{n-1} + b_{n-1}$$
$$b_n = a_{n-1} + c_{n-1}$$
$$c_n = a_{n-1}$$

Therefore,

$$a_4 = 18, b_4 = 12, c_4 = 6$$
$$a_5 = 30, b_5 = 24, c_5 = 18$$
$$a_6 = 54, b_6 = 48, c_6 = 30$$
$$a_7 = 102, b_7 = 84, c_7 = 54$$

Hence, there are $a_7 + b_7 + c_7 = 240$ number of sequences satisfying the given condition.

5. (B)

Let a_n be the number of n-strings that ends with H and b_n be the number of n-strings that ends with M. Hence, $a_n = b_{n-1} + b_{n-2}$ and $b_n = b_{n-1} + a_{n-1}$. Therefore, $(a_i, b_i)_{i \in \mathbb{N}} = (1, 1), (2, 2), (3, 4), (6, 7), (11, 13), (20, 24), (37, 44), (68, 81), (125, 149), (230, 274), \cdots$. Hence, $a_{10} + b_{10} = 504$.

6. (E)

Let a_n be the number of n-strings that ends with 1, b_n that ends with 2, c_n that ends with 3, d_n that ends with 4, e_n that ends with 5 and f_n that ends with 6. Then, according to the given condition,

$$a_n = a_{n-1}$$
$$b_n = a_{n-1} + b_{n-1}$$
$$c_n = a_{n-1} + b_{n-1} + c_{n-1}$$
$$d_n = a_{n-1} + b_{n-1} + c_{n-1} + d_{n-1}$$
$$e_n = a_{n-1} + b_{n-1} + c_{n-1} + d_{n-1} + e_{n-1}$$
$$f_n = a_{n-1} + b_{n-1} + c_{n-1} + d_{n-1} + e_{n-1} + f_{n-1}$$

Hence, $(a_i, b_i, c_i, d_i, e_i, f_i)_{i\in\mathbb{N}} = (1,1,1,1,1,1), (1,2,3,4,5,6), (1,3,6,10,15,21),$ $(1,4,10,20,35,56), \cdots$. Hence, there are 126 number of sequences of size 4-strings.

On the other hand, we could have solved the same problem using "circles and bars." In particular, let a be the face value that appears in the first roll, b that appears in the second roll, c that appears in the third roll, and d that appears in the fourth roll. According to the given condition, we have $1 \leq a \leq b \leq c \leq d \leq 6$. This naturally brings forth "circles and bars." Let x_1 be the number of appearances of 1 in (a,b,c,d), x_2 that of 2 in (a,b,c,d), x_3 that of 3 in (a,b,c,d), $\cdots$, and x_6 that of 6 in (a,b,c,d). Then,

$$x_1 + x_2 + x_3 + x_4 + x_5 + x_6 = 4$$

Hence, by circles and bars, we get $\binom{9}{4} = 126$.

7. (E)

As a whole, we could have computed as F_n where F_n counts the number of n-strings satisfying the given condition. Then, we get $F_n = F_{n-1} + F_{n-2}$ by looking at the last terms.

On the other hand, we could have gone through caseworks. In particular, if a_n is the number of n-strings that ends with a 1×1 block and b_n is the number of n-strings that ends with a 1×2 block, then $a_n = a_{n-1} + b_{n-1}$ and $b_n = a_{n-2} + b_{n-2}$. However, $a_n + b_n = (a_{n-1} + b_{n-1}) + (a_{n-2} + b_{n-2})$ and $F_n = F_{n-1} + F_{n-2}$ are not different. The base cases of F_n are $F_1 = 1$ and $F_2 = 2$. Hence, $F_{i\in\mathbb{N}} = 1, 2, 3, 5, 8, 13, 21, 34, 55, 89, 144$.

8. (B)

Color all regions as fixed, i.e., 6!. Now, get rid of all overcounts by fixing a vertex in 8 different ways and rotate it 120°, 240° or 360°. Hence, we get

$$\frac{6!}{8 \times 3} = 30$$

different number of coloring a cube using six different colors.

9. (D)

Let's solve the problem by using casework. Let B be the number of faces that are colored blue and G the number of faces that are colored green. Then, $B + G = 6$ implies that

- $(B, G) = (6, 0)$ implies that there is 1 way to color the cube.
- $(B, G) = (5, 1)$ implies that there is 1 way to color the cube.
- $(B, G) = (4, 2)$ implies that there are 2 ways to color the cube.
- $(B, G) = (3, 3)$ implies that there are 2 ways to color the cube.
- $(B, G) = (2, 4)$ implies that there are 2 ways to color the cube.
- $(B, G) = (1, 5)$ implies that there are 1 way to color the cube.
- $(B, G) = (0, 6)$ implies that there is 1 way to color the cube.

Adding it all up, we get 10 number of different ways to color the cube. On the other hand, we may use Burnside lemma. The Burnside lemma fixes the figure in terms of distinct transformation done to the figure, adds all the sum of permuting colors in all regions allowing repetition, and divides the total sum by the number of all different transformations done to the cube. Have a look at the following illustration.

- Identity : Since there are 6 different places that can be colored using two colors, there are 2^6 number of ways to color the cube.
- x, y, and z-axis rotation : Rotating the cube along one of the axes by 90° produces 3 different places to color using two colors. Since there are three different places to color using two colors, we get 2^3 number of ways to color the cube when it is rotated by 90°. Rotating it along one of the axes by 180° produces 4 different places to color using two colors. Since there are four different places to color using two colors, we get 2^4 number of ways to color the cube when it is rotated by 180°. Lastly, rotating it along one of the axes by 270° produces 3 different places to color using two colors. Since there are three different places to color using two colors, we get 2^3 number of ways to color the cube when it is rotated by 270°. In other words, we have $3 \times (2^3 + 2^4 + 2^3)$ number of ways to color the cube.

- Diagonal rotation : Fix a digonal of a cube. In fact, there are 4 diagonals in total. Now, given a diagonal, imagine rotating the cube about 120° and 240°. Rotating it 360° has been counted in the first casework of "identity," so we count 8 number of transformations. For 120° rotation about the diagonal, there are only two different places to color using two colors. Likewise, for 240° rotationa bout the diagonal, there are two different places to color using two colors, as well. Hence, there are 8×2^2 number of ways to color the cube.

- Remaining axes : Consider a pair of opposite sides of a cube. Connect the midpoints of the two edges, a line of which passes through the center of the cube. There are six lines in total. In each axis, there are three different places to color using two colors. Hence, there are 6×2^3 number of ways to color the cube.

In total, according to Burnside lemma, we get

$$\frac{2^6 + 3(2^3 + 2^4 + 2^3) + 8(2^2) + 6(2^3)}{24} = 10$$

10. (C)

Let's directly use Burnside lemma.

- Identity : 3^6 ways to color a cube. In particular, there are six different places to color using three colors, so there must be 3^6 ways to color the cube.

- x, y, and z-axes : $3 \times (3^3 + 3^4 + 3^3)$ ways to color a cube. It follows the same logical process illustrated in the previous question. For 90° rotation along one of the axes, there are three places to color using three colors in 3^3 number of ways. Likewise, 180° rotation along one of the axes results in four different places to color using three colors in 3^4 number of ways. Lastly, 270° rotation along one of the axes results in three different places to color using three colors in 3^3 number of ways.

- Diagonal rotation : 8×3^2 ways to color a cube, since diagonal rotation about 120° or 240° produces two regions to color.

- Unseen rotation : 6×3^3 ways to color a cube, since diagonal rotation about 180° produces three regions to color.

Hence, there are $\dfrac{3^6 + 3(3^3 + 3^4 + 3^3) + 8 \cdot 3^2 + 6 \cdot 3^3}{24} = 57$ ways.

11. (B)

Use Burnside lemma.

- Identity : 2^9 ways to color a square.

- 90° rotation : 2^3 ways to color a square.

- 180° rotation : 2^5 ways to color a square.

- 270° rotation : 2^3 ways to color a square.

- Reflection about the vertical line passing through the center : 2^6 ways to color a square.

- Reflection about the horizontal line passing through the center : 2^6 ways to color a square.

- Reflection about a diagonal line passing through the center : 2^6 ways to color a square.

- Reflection about another diagonal line passing through the center : 2^6 ways to color a square.

Hence,
$$\frac{2^9 + 2^3 + 2^5 + 2^3 + 2^6 + 2^6 + 2^6 + 2^6}{8} = 102$$

12. (D)

Use Burnside lemma.

- Identity : $\binom{9}{3} = 84$ ways to color a square.

- 90° rotation : no way to color a square.

- 180° rotation : 4 ways to color a square.

- 270° rotation : no way to color a square.

- Reflection about the vertical line passing through the center : 10 ways to color a square.

- Reflection about the horizontal line passing through the center : 10 ways to color a square.

- Reflection about a diagonal line passing through the center : 10 ways to color a square.

- Reflection about another diagonal line passing through the center : 10 ways to color a square.

Hence,
$$\frac{84 + 0 + 4 + 10 + 10 + 10 + 10}{8} = 16$$

Or, we can perform caseworks on a fixed 3×3 square labeled each small square with 1 through 9 such as

1	2	3
4	5	6
7	8	9

Then, color three greens at $(1,2,3)$, $(1,2,4)$, $(1,2,6)$, $(1,2,7)$, $(1,2,8)$, $(1,2,9)$, $(1,3,7)$, $(1,3,8)$, $(2,4,5)$, $(2,5,8)$, $(1,5,9)$, $(1,4,5)$, $(1,5,6)$, $(1,3,5)$, $(2,4,6)$, and $(2,6,7)$, which are all different. Hence, there are 16 distinct ways of coloring a 3×3 square.

13. (A)
Let E be the expected number of times Bob will roll a die in a day. Then, $E = \frac{2}{6} \times 1 + \frac{4}{6} \times (1 + E)$, so $E = 3$. Each day, the expected number of times Bob will roll a die is 3. Hence, by linearity of expectation, the average number of throws must be $30 \times 3 = 90$.

14. (B)
Let the indicator variable be 1 if the given spot is unchanged and 0 if the given spot is changed. The probability of getting 1 is $\frac{2}{6}$ and that of getting 0 is $\frac{4}{6}$. By linearity of expectation, we get

$$(1 \times \frac{2}{6} + 0 \times \frac{4}{6}) + (1 \times \frac{2}{6} + 0 \times \frac{4}{6}) + \cdots + (1 \times \frac{2}{6} + 0 \times \frac{4}{6}) = 6$$

15. (D)
Let the indicator variable be 1 if a chosen card is between ace of spade or heart, and 0 if otherwise. Hence, by linearity of expectation, $50 \times (1 \times \frac{1}{3} + 0 \times \frac{2}{3}) = \frac{50}{3}$. Hence, $m + n = 53$.

16. (C)
Let the indicator variable be 1 if the three consecutive spots have different numbers and 0 otherwise. Since there are 99 3-length strings with the probability of satisfying the condition as $2/9 = 3!/3^3$, we get $E = 99(1 \cdot \frac{2}{9} + 0 \cdot \frac{7}{9}) = 22$ number of 3-length strings of all different numbers in a string of 101 numbers.

17. (B)

Let's define indicator variable on each 2-string such that it is 1 if is either 00 or 11, and 0 otherwise. Since there are 7 strings in total, by linearity of expected value, we compute it as

$$7 \times (1 \times \frac{2}{4} + 0 \times \frac{2}{4}) = \frac{7}{2}$$

Hence, $m + n = 9$.

18. (D)

Define indicator variable on each rectangle such that it is 1 if it's vertex-monochromatic and 0 otherwise. Since there $100 (= \binom{5}{2} \cdot \binom{5}{2})$ number of rectangles, we use the linearity of expected value to compute m/n as

$$100 \times (1 \times \frac{3}{3^4} + 0 \times \frac{78}{3^4}) = \frac{100}{27}$$

Hence, $m + n = 127$.

19. (C)

Let E_x be the number of steps required to go from one of the four vertices of a 2×2 square to the center for the first time and E_y be the number of steps required to reach the center for the first time from four dots in the edges. Then, we can easily set up equations for random-walk. For E_x, there are two possible routes to dots labeled as E_y. We add 1 to the equation since 1 step is used to reach dots with E_y from vertices with E_x.

Use similar approach to E_y to find out the equation in terms of E_x. There are two routes back to vertices with E_x and 1 route to the center dot. Hence, we can write down two equations, i.e.,

$$E_x = E_y + 1$$
$$E_y = \frac{1}{3}(1) + \frac{2}{3}(1 + E_x)$$

Solving the system of equations, we get $E_x = 6$ and $E_y = 5$. Therefore, the product of E_x and E_y is 30.

20. (A)

Let E_x be the expected number of steps from the vertices of a cube, E_y be the expected number of steps from the dots on the center of the edges, and E_z be the expected number of steps from center dots on each face. Then, using similar logic as in the previous question, we get

$$E_x = E_y + 1$$
$$E_y = \frac{1}{2}(E_x + 1) + \frac{1}{2}(E_z + 1)$$
$$E_z = \frac{1}{5}(1) + \frac{4}{5}(E_y + 1)$$

Hence, $E_x = 21$, solving the equation.

Math Competitions for Highschool Students

Here is the list of math competitions for which highschool students can apply.

- American Mathematics Competitions (also known as AMC) : AMC 10 , AMC 12 , AIME , USAJMO , USAMO

- American Regions Math League (ARML)

- Math League

- Purple Comet! Math Meet (PCMM)

- Rocket City Math League (RCML)

- Math Prize for Girls

- Spirit of Math & Stanford SMILE Competition

- Harvard MIT Math Tournament (HMMT)

- Stanford Math Tournament (SMT)

- Berkeley Math Tournament (BMT)

- Rice Math Tournament (RMT)

- The Princeton University Math Competition (PUMaC)

- Carnegie Mellon Informatics and Mathematics Competition (CMIMC)

- Johns Hopkins Mathematics Tournament (JHMT)

- Canadian Open Mathematics Challenge (COMC)

- Caribou Mathematics Competition

- USA Mathematical Talent Search (USAMTS)

TOPIC 5

Mixed Practice

Practice

1. (1-to-1 Correspondence)

Let A be the number of appearances of 5, out of integers between 1 and 9999, inclusive, and B be the number of integers that contains at least one 5. Find the difference between A and B.

(A) 560

(B) 561

(C) 562

(D) 563

(E) 564

2. (Casework)

Find the number of all natural triples (x, y, z) satisfying $3x + 2y + z = 12$.

(A) 5

(B) 6

(C) 7

(D) 8

(E) 9

3. (Partition of ℕ)

How many ways are there to partition 10 into 3 natural numbers?

(A) 5
(B) 6
(C) 7
(D) 8
(E) 9

4. (Triangular Inequality and Casework)

How many triangles are there whose perimeter is 24 with side lengths x, y, z all integers? (If triangles are congruent, they are considered equal.)

(A) 10
(B) 11
(C) 12
(D) 13
(E) 14

5. (Casework + Partition of Natural Numbers)

As shown in the diagram below, the two parallel lines are apart with the distance of 1 unit, where each dot is 1 unit away from adjacent points. How many ways are there to choose four points so that the area of a quadrilateral formed by connecting the four points is 4 in the following diagram?

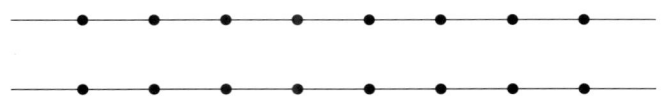

(A) 84
(B) 88
(C) 92
(D) 96
(E) 100

6. (Casework)

Let x and y be positive integers such that x is even and y is a positive multiple of x. If $x + y = 500$, compute the number of distinct ordered pairs of (x, y).

(A) 6
(B) 7
(C) 8
(D) 9
(E) 10

7. (Derangement)

How many different arrangements of distinct one-digit primes are there such that the first digit cannot be 2, the second cannot be 3, the third cannot be 5 and the last cannot be 7?

(A) 8
(B) 9
(C) 10
(D) 11
(E) 12

8. (Derangement)

Allen, Brian, Colin, David and Emily form a team of mathletes prepping for a math competition. Allen, a leader of the team, suggested an idea of taking an individual mock exam written by one another. All team members received one test written by others. How many ways are there for these five mathletes to take mock exams?

(A) 40
(B) 42
(C) 44
(D) 46
(E) 48

9. (Recursion)

If there are 8 steps in a staircase, where Bob the long-legged can step up only by 1 step, 2 steps and 3 steps at once, how many ways are there for Bob to go up on a staircase from the bottom to top?

(A) 79
(B) 80
(C) 81
(D) 82
(E) 83

10. (Distinct marbles in Distinct plates)

Given a set $U = \{x_1, x_2, x_3, \cdots, x_{2020}, x_{2021}\}$, if $X \subset Y \subset U$ for subsets X, Y of U, the number of pairs (X, Y) can be written as n^p where n is a prime. Find $n + p$.

(A) 2021
(B) 2022
(C) 2023
(D) 2024
(E) 2025

11. (Counting in Number Theory)

When the greatest common divisor and least common multiple of two positive integers are multiplied, their product is $1,350,000$. How many different values could be the greatest common divisor of the two integers?

(A) 12
(B) 14
(C) 16
(D) 18
(E) 20

12. (Function with Conditions)

Given a set $U = \{1, 2, 3, 4, 5, 6, \cdots, 2021\}$, if $f : U \longrightarrow U$ is a function from U to U, the number of functions f such that

$$f(1) - 1 = f(2) - 2 = f(3) - 3 = f(4) - 4 = \cdots = f(2019) - 2019$$

can be written as $m \times p^r \times q^s$ where m, r, and s are positive integers, and p and q are primes. Find $m + p + r + q + s$.

(A) 89
(B) 91
(C) 93
(D) 95
(E) 97

13. (Function with Conditions)

There is a set $U = \{1, 2, 3, 4, 5, \cdots, 100\}$. Assume that two subsets X and Y satisfy $X \setminus Y = \{p \in \mathbb{N} : \text{p is a prime less than or equal to 100}\}$. If the number of all possible pairs of (X, Y) can be written as p^q where p is a prime number and q is an integer, find $p \times q$.

(A) 75

(B) 150

(C) 225

(D) 250

(E) 275

14. (Counting with Restrictions)

Given integers a, b, c, and d, in how many distinct quadruples of (a, b, c, d) is the condition $|a| + |b| + |c| + |d| = 4$ satisfied?

(A) 188

(B) 190

(C) 192

(D) 194

(E) 196

15. (Counting with Restrictions)

Given integers a, b, c, and d, in how many quadruples (a, b, c, d) is the condition such that $a^2 + b^2 + c^2 + d^2 = 25$ and at least one of the integers is 0 satisfied?

(A) 52

(B) 56

(C) 60

(D) 64

(E) 68

16. (Getting rid of Overcounts)

There are five students, Amy, Brian, Cory, Daniel and Ewan. In how many arrangements will they form a line from left to right such that Amy must be left of Brian and Cory, while Daniel and Ewan must be set apart?

(A) 18

(B) 24

(C) 30

(D) 36

(E) 42

17. (Counting with Overcounts)

$$\boxed{A|A|A|B|B|C|C|C}$$

As shown in the figure above, national representatives from Australia, Bulgaria and Croatia are seated in a row of eight seats. Find the number of arrangements of all eight representatives such that all three delegates from Australia are left of those from Croatia.

(A) 2014
(B) 2016
(C) 2018
(D) 2020
(E) 2022

18. (Partition of Sets)

There are seven people in front of a lobby elevator at four-story Hotel Math. The lift is so old that at most five people can be in the elevator. In how many ways can the five people get off the lift at 2nd, 3rd or 4th floor, assuming that there is no one left behind, and it is possible that everyone leaves at the same floor?

(A) 5100
(B) 5103
(C) 5106
(D) 5109
(E) 5112

19. (Geometric Counting)

How many non-degenerate "squares" can be drawn, using four points in the figure?

· · · ·

· · · ·

· · · ·

· · · ·

(A) 14
(B) 16
(C) 18
(D) 20
(E) 22

20. (Geometric Counting)

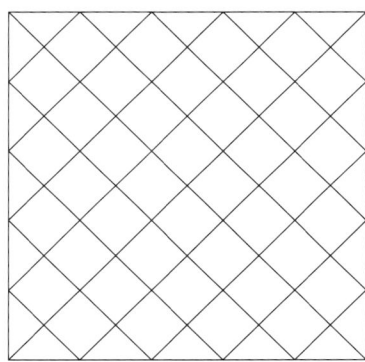

How many squares appear in the diagram below?
(A) 82
(B) 83
(C) 84
(D) 85
(E) 86

21. (Standard Casework + Complementary Counting)

How many four-digit positive integers are multiples of 3 with at least one digit of 1?

(A) 1057
(B) 1059
(C) 1061
(D) 1063
(E) 1065

22. (Clever Casework)

The number of natural numbers smaller than or equal to 99,999 that include exactly two digits of 5 can be written as $p^a q^b r^c$ where p, q and r are prime integers. Find $p + q + r + a + b + c$.

(A) 15
(B) 16
(C) 17
(D) 18
(E) 19

23. (Principle of Inclusion and Exclusion)

How many multiples of 2 or 3 or 5, but not of 7, are there between 1 and 1000, inclusive?

(A) 620

(B) 625

(C) 630

(D) 635

(E) 640

24. (Subset)

Let $X = \{x \in \mathbb{Z} : x = 2^a \times 3^b \times 5^c\}$ where a, b, and c are non-negative integers. How many subsets of $Y = \{x : x \in X \text{ and } 1 < x \leq 20\}$ such that it includes every multiple of 5 and at least one perfect squares?

(A) 444

(B) 448

(C) 452

(D) 456

(E) 460

25. (Distinctive or Not)

How many five-digit numbers are there, if 5 digits are selected from

$$\{2, 2, 2, 3, 3, 3, 5, 5, 7\}$$

?

(A) 490
(B) 500
(C) 510
(D) 520
(E) 530

26. (Clever Summation)

Given a set of first ten prime numbers, $\{2, 3, 5, 7, 11, 13, 17, 19, 23, 29\}$, if there are n subsets with three distinct elements, then the sum of all elements in n sets can be written as the product of primes in the list and other prime not in the list. Find the other prime.

(A) 31
(B) 37
(C) 41
(D) 43
(E) 47

27. (Group Counts)

Assume there exists an infinite decimal expression whose expression is written in increasing order without any jump, i.e.,

$$0.123456789101112\cdots 201920202021\cdots$$

Find out the 2021st digit under decimal point.

(A) 0
(B) 1
(C) 2
(D) 3
(E) 4

28. (Geometric Counting)

If there is a regular hexagon with one vertex labeled as X and its opposite vertex as Y, assume that there is an ant called "Bob" at X that moves along the edge per minute. In how many ways can Bob be placed at Y exactly after 7 minutes?

(A) 14
(B) 21
(C) 35
(D) 42
(E) 70

29. (Empty Spaces)

Suppose there are twelve empty seats in a row. If four seats for "seat separation" are to selected out of these chairs, in how many ways can the four seats be selected if there should be at least one empty seat in both sides of the chosen empty seats?

(A) 21
(B) 35
(C) 42
(D) 70
(E) 84

30. (Adjacency)

$$\boxed{R|S|R|R|S|R|S|T|S|T|S|T|T|T|T}$$

As shown in the diagram above, there are four Rs, five Ss, and six Ts. The largest perfect square that divides the number of arrangements such that all Ss are not adjacent to one another can be written as n^2. Find the value of $|n|$.

(A) 3
(B) 7
(C) 21
(D) 42
(E) 63

31. (Separation)

If we select three distinct numbers from $\{1, 2, 3, 4, \cdots, 21\}$, in how many ways are there such that any two pair has the difference of at least 5?

(A) 228

(B) 244

(C) 260

(D) 275

(E) 286

32. (Condition)

Out of 4-digit numbers, if the units digit is 2, how many numbers have exactly two equal digits?

(A) 360

(B) 384

(C) 392

(D) 404

(E) 426

33. (Circular Permutation + Partition of $\mathbb{N}$)

How many ways are there to arrange ten black marbles and three white marbles around a round table? Two arrangements are considered identical if one image is a rotation of another.

(A) 6
(B) 10
(C) 14
(D) 18
(E) 22

34. (Circular Permutation with Condition)

There are seven people, including two supervisors, seated around a round table. How many ways are there to arrange these members such that there is at least one person between supervisors?

(A) 120
(B) 240
(C) 360
(D) 480
(E) 600

35. (Circles and Bars)

Find the number of natural number triples (x, y, z) such that $x + y + z < 20$.

(A) 455

(B) 560

(C) 680

(D) 816

(E) 969

36. (Complement and Combination allowing repetitions)

How many 6-tuples of (a, b, c, d, e, f) where a, b, c, d, e, and f are non-negative integers satisfy the following two properties?

- $a + b + c + d + e + f = 15$

- $2^a \cdot 4^b$ is a multiple of 4, or $3^c \cdot 9^d$ is a multiple of 9.

(A) 14641

(B) 15444

(C) 15500

(D) 15765

(E) 16215

37. (Combination allowing repetitions and Number Theory)

Find the number of positive integers smaller than or equal to $999,999$ such that the sum of the digits equals 9.

(A) 2000

(B) 2001

(C) 2002

(D) 2003

(E) 2004

38. (Multiplication Principle)

If the number of configurations for three adults and six students to be seated at a movie theater with three rows with four seats such that there should be one adult in each row can be uniquely expressed as a prime factorization form $p_1^{q_1} p_2^{q_2} \cdots p_k^{q_k}$ where $k \geq 2$, compute the sum $\sum_{i=1}^{k} (p_i + q_i)$.

(A) 34

(B) 35

(C) 36

(D) 37

(E) 38

39. (Multiplication Principle)

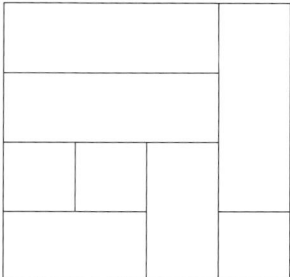

If all regions laid out in the figure above are painted using four different types - yellow, green, purple, and blue, the following five conditions must be satisfied.

- Each of the color must be used at least once.

- Adjacent regions CAN be colored with the same color.

- The number of regions with yellow color is at least that with green color.

- The number of regions with green color is at least that with purple color.

- The number of regions with purple color is at least that with blue color.

If there are n distinct configurations, how many distinct digits does n have?

(A) 1
(B) 2
(C) 3
(D) 4
(E) 5

40. (Matching Condition coupled with Derangement)

There are ten different lockers with ten distinct keys. In particular, a specific key opens up only one locker. Otherwise, it will not open. If only four keys open the lockers and other six keys fail to pen the lockers in n different ways, compute the number of distinct prime factors of n.

(A) 3

(B) 4

(C) 5

(D) 6

(E) 7

41. (Constructive Counting)

Suppose there are five couples attending an entertainment show. If a show host picks five people at random, in how many arrangements are there such that there is only one whole couple not picked by the host?

(A) 80

(B) 120

(C) 140

(D) 160

(E) 180

42. (Tournament)

Suppose there are 8 mathletes, any two of which do not tie. Regardless of their own faculties, the win or loss are determined by their given ranks. The first best player always wins against any other players. If they play up on a tournament, in how many arrangements are there such that the third best player will play at the final round?

(A) 60

(B) 90

(C) 120

(D) 150

(E) 180

43. (Binomial Theorem)

If $(\sqrt{1} + \sqrt{3} + \sqrt{5})^5 = p + \sqrt{q} + \sqrt{r} + \sqrt{t}$ where p, q, r, and t are integers such that q, r, and t are not perfect squares, find the value of p.

(A) 651

(B) 701

(C) 771

(D) 831

(E) 871

44. (Combination allowing repetition)

If Bob throws an unbiased die four times in a row, in how many configurations will the numbers that show up in four throws are not decreasing?

(A) 84
(B) 100
(C) 126
(D) 144
(E) 165

45. (Parity)

Suppose there are 30 seats in a row, and 8 identical-looking marbles on top of some 8 chairs. If there are odd number of chairs between any consecutive pair of chairs with marbles, the number of possible arrangements of 8 marbles can be written as $p \times \binom{n}{k}$, where $k \geq 8$. Compute $p + n + k$.

(A) 23
(B) 24
(C) 25
(D) 26
(E) 27

Solution

1. The answer is (B). We casework to find out that 5 appears $10^3 \times 4 = 4000$ times. On the other hand, the number of integers that contains at least one 5 is equal to $9^3 \times 4 + 9^2 \times \binom{4}{2} + 9 \times 4 + 1 = 3439$. Hence, $A = 4000$ and $B = 3439$. Therefore, $A - B = 561$.

2. The answer is (C). We perform casework on x. If $x = 1$, then $2y + z = 9$. Hence, there are four pairs of (y, z) for $x = 1$. If $x = 2$, then $2y + z = 6$. Hence, there are two pairs of (y, z) for $x = 2$. If $x = 3$, then $2y + z = 3$. Hence, there is one pair of (y, z) for $x = 3$. Therefore, there are 7 triples.

3. The answer is (D).

$$a + b + c = 10$$
$$8 + 1 + 1 = 10$$
$$7 + 2 + 1 = 10$$
$$6 + 3 + 1 = 10$$
$$5 + 4 + 1 = 10$$
$$6 + 2 + 2 = 10$$
$$5 + 3 + 2 = 10$$
$$4 + 4 + 2 = 10$$
$$4 + 3 + 3 = 10$$

4. The answer is (C). Let $x \geq y \geq z$. Then $x + y + z = 24$. By triangular inequality, $x < y + z$ implies that $x < 12$. On the other hand, by the first assumption, $8 \leq x$. Hence, $x = 8, 9, 10, 11$. If $x = 8$, then $(y, z) = (8, 8)$. If $x = 9$, then $(y, z) = (9, 6), (8, 7)$. If $x = 10$, then $(y, z) = (10, 4), (9, 5), (8, 6), (7, 7)$. If $x = 10$, then $(y, z) = (11, 2), (10, 3), (9, 4), (8, 5), (7, 6)$. Hence, there are 12 non-congruent triangles with integer side lengths.

5. The answer is (A). Let a be the length of the segment on the top row and b be that on the bottom row. Then, $a + b = 8$ implies that $(a, b) = (7, 1), (6, 2), (5, 3), \cdots, (1, 6)$. If $(a, b) = (7, 1)$, then there are 1×7 possible ways of choosing segments. if $(a, b) = (6, 2)$, then there are 2×6 possible ways of choosing segments. Keep continuing this process until $(a, b) = (1, 7)$ where there are 7×1 possible ways of choosing segments. Hence, the sum of all possible arrangements of segment selections equals 84.

6. The answer is (B). Let $x = 2k$ for some positive integer k. Then, $y = 2kk'$ where k' is some positive integer k'. Hence,

$$x + y = 500$$
$$2k + 2kk' = 500$$
$$2k(1 + k') = 500$$
$$k(1 + k') = 250$$

where $k \geq 1$ and $k' \geq 1$. Notice that $(k, 1+k') = (125, 2), (50, 5), (25, 10), (10, 25), (5, 50), (2, 125)$, and $(1, 250)$. Check that $(k, 1+k') = (250, 1)$ is excluded from the list, since $1 + k' \geq 2$ where $k' \geq 1$. Therefore, there are 7 ordered pairs of (x, y) satisfying the given condition.

7. The answer is (B). This is a typical problem related to derangement. Using the principle of inclusion and exclusion,

$$\frac{4!}{2!} - \frac{4!}{3!} + \frac{4!}{4!} = 12 - 4 + 1 = 9$$

Or, we could use the formula $D_n = n! \sum_{k=2}^{n} \frac{(-1)^k}{k!}$, where D_n counts the number of derangements of n different letters, to compute $D_4 = 9$.

8. The answer is (C). This is a word problem which uses derangement. Using the principle of inclusion and exclusion,

$$\frac{5!}{2!} - \frac{5!}{3!} + \frac{5!}{4!} - \frac{5!}{5!} = 60 - 20 + 5 - 1 = 44$$

9. The answer is (C). Let F_n be the number of ways for Bob to climb n steps in total. Then,

$$\{F_i\}_{i \in \mathbb{N}} = \{1, 2, 4, 7, 13, 24, 44, 81, \cdots\}$$

10. The answer is (D). For x_i where $1 \leq i \leq 2021$ and i is an integer, x_i can be in X, $Y \setminus X$ or $U \setminus Y$. Hence, there are 3 possibilities for x_i to be placed in the Venn Diagram with $X \subset Y \subset U$. Hence, by the principle of multiplication, we have 3^{2021} possible ways to place x_i in the proper regions, and we have 1-to-1 correspondence with (X, Y). Thus, the answer is (D).

11. The answer is (D). Let a and b be two positive integers, then the product of greatest common divisor and least common multiple equals the product of a and b, so $ab = 1,350,000 = 2^4 \times 3^3 \times 5^5$. Now, let $a = 2^r 3^s 5^t$ and $b = 2^x 3^y 5^z$. Then, $r + x = 4$, $s + y = 3$ and $t + z = 5$. Since $(r, x) = (4, 0), (3, 1), (2, 2), (1, 3), (0, 4)$, the minimum of $\{r, x\}$ equals 0, 1, or 2. Likewise, since $(s, y) = (3, 0), (2, 1), (1, 2), (0, 3)$, the minimum of $\{s, y\}$ equals 0 or 1. Lastly, since $(t, z) = (5, 0), (4, 1), (3, 2), (2, 3), (1, 4), (0, 5)$, the minimum of $\{t, z\}$ equals 0, 1, or 2. Therefore, the number of greatest common factor of a and b is $18 (= 3 \times 2 \times 3)$.

12. The answer is (E). There are three possible cases to work on. Let $f(1) - 1 = \cdots = f(2019) - 2019 = 0$. Also, $f(2020) \in \{1, 2, 3, \cdots, 2021\}$ and $f(2021) \in \{1, 2, 3, \cdots, 2021\}$ implies that $1^{2019} \times 2021 \times 2021$. Likewise, let $f(1) - 1 = \cdots = f(2019) - 2019 = 1$. Apply a similar logic to this case as well, to get $1^{2019} \times 2021^2$. Lastly, let $f(1) - 1 = f(2) - 2 = \cdots = f(2019) - 2019 = 2$. We also get $1^{2019} \times 2021^2$ in this last case. Hence, there are $3 \times 2021^2 = 3 \times 43^2 \times 47^2$. Thus, $m + p + r + q + s = 97$.

13. The answer is (C). There are 25 primes less than or equal to 100, i.e., 2, 3, 5, 7, 11, 13, 17, 19, 23, 29, 31, 37, 41, 43, 47, 53, 59, 61, 67, 71, 73, 79, 83, 89, and 97. Then, there are 75 integers to be placed in $X \cap Y$, $Y \setminus X$ and $U \setminus (X \cup Y)$. Hence, there are 3^{75} possible ways to place each number and we have 1-to-1 correspondence with the number of (X, Y) with the arrangements of integers into respective places in Venn Diagram.

14. The answer is (C). First, use partition of natural numbers to produce four possible cases.

$$|a| + |b| + |c| + |d| = 4 + 0 + 0 + 0$$
$$= 3 + 1 + 0 + 0$$
$$= 2 + 2 + 0 + 0$$
$$= 2 + 1 + 1 + 0$$
$$= 1 + 1 + 1 + 1$$

Now, we investigate each case in detail.

- $4+0+0+0$ has $4 \times 2^1 = 8$ different arrangements.
- $3+1+0+0$ has $\frac{4!}{2!} \times 2^2 = 48$ different arrangements.
- $2+2+0+0$ has $\frac{4!}{2!2!} \times 2^2 = 24$ different arrangements.
- $2+1+1+0$ has $\frac{4!}{2!} \times 2^3 = 96$ different arrangements.
- $1+1+1+1$ has $2^4 = 16$ different arrangements.

Hence, there are $192(= 8+48+24+96+16)$ different quadruples satisfying $|a|+|b|+|c|+|d|=4$.

15. The answer is (B). First, use partition of natural numbers to produce four possible cases.

$$a^2+b^2+c^2+d^2 = 25+0+0+0$$
$$= 16+9+0+0$$
$$= 16+4+4+1$$

Since there is another condition stating that there is at least one 0 in the quadruple, the last case must be eliminated. Now, we investigate each case in detail.

- $25+0+0+0$ has $4 \times 2^1 = 8$ different arrangements.
- $16+9+0+0$ has $\frac{4!}{2!} \times 2^2 = 48$ different arrangements.

Hence, there are $56(=8+48)$ different quadruples satisfying $a^2+b^2+c^2+d^2=25$.

16. The answer is (B). First, Daniel and Ewan can be placed apart in $\binom{4}{2} \times 2!$ number of ways. Second, Amy, Brian and Cory can be placed in (A,B,C) or (A,C,B). Hence, we get $\binom{4}{2} \times 2! \times 2 = 24$.

17. The answer is (B). Out of any possible arrangement of A's, B's, and C's, notice that the order between A's and C's must be $AAACCC$. Then, the total number of arrangements satisfying the given condition must be

$$\frac{8!}{6!} \times 3!3! = 2016$$

18. The answer is (B). First, choose 5 people out of 7 people, i.e, $\binom{7}{5}$. Then, each selected individual has 3 floors to choose, so there are $\binom{7}{5} \times 3^5 = 5103$ ways to choose five people to get off the lift at 2nd, 3rd and 4th floor, leaving no one behind.

19. The answer is (D). There are 9 squares of area 1. There are 4 squares of area 2. There are 4 squares of area 4. There are 2 squares of area 5. There is 1 square of area 9. Hence, there are 20 squares in total.

20. The answer is (B). There are 40 1×1 squares. There are 25 2×2 squares. There are 12 3×3 squares. There are 5 4×4 squares. Lastly, there is a biggest square. Hence, there are 83 squares in the figure.

21. The answer is (B). First off, there are 3000 four-digit multiples of 3. Now, it's time to get rid of multiples of 3 without using 1 as its digit. Let $\overline{abcd}$ be a four-digit number. Then, perform casework.

- If $a = \{2, 5, 8\}$, then $b + c + d \equiv 1 \pmod 3$. Hence, $(b, c, d) \equiv (1, 0, 0), (0, 1, 0), (0, 0, 1), (2, 2, 0), (2, 0, 2), (0, 2, 2), (2, 1, 1), (1, 2, 1), (1, 1, 2) \pmod 3$. Therefore, there are $3 \times (3 \times 2 \times 4 \times 4 + 3 \times 4 \times 3 \times 3 + 3 \times 3 \times 2 \times 2) = 720$ possible cases.

- If $a = \{4, 7\}$, then $b + c + d \equiv 2 \pmod 3$. Hence, $(b, c, d) \equiv (2, 0, 0), (2, 0, 0), (0, 0, 2), (1, 1, 0), (1, 0, 1), (0, 1, 1), (2, 2, 1), (2, 1, 2), (1, 2, 2) \pmod 3$. There are $2 \times (3 \times 4 \times 4 \times 3 + 2 \times 2 \times 4 \times 3 + 3 \times 3 \times 2 \times 3) = 492$ possible cases.

- If $a = \{3, 6, 9\}$, then $b + c + d \equiv 0 \pmod 3$. Hence, $(b, c, d) \equiv (0, 0, 0), (1, 1, 1), (2, 2, 2), (1, 2, 0), (1, 0, 2), (0, 1, 2), (0, 2, 1), (2, 0, 1), (2, 1, 0) \pmod 3$. There are $3 \times (4^3 + 2^3 + 3^3 + 3! \times 2 \times 3 \times 4) = 729$ possible cases.

Using complementary counting, get rid of $1941 (= 720 + 492 + 729)$ numbers from 3000 numbers. Hence, there are 1059 four-digit multiples of 3 containing at least one 1.

22. The answer is (D). There are $\binom{5}{2}$ places to place two 5's in five possible digits, and 9^3 ways to fill the three empty digits, including 0. Hence, $\binom{5}{2} \times 9^3 = 10 \times 9^3 = 2^1 3^6 5^1$. Therefore, $p + q + r + a + b + c = 2 + 3 + 5 + 1 + 6 + 1 = 18$.

23. The answer is (C). Let's compute the number of positive multiples of 2, 3, or 5 smaller than or equal to 1000, i.e.,

$$\lfloor \frac{1000}{2} \rfloor + \lfloor \frac{1000}{3} \rfloor + \lfloor \frac{1000}{5} \rfloor - \lfloor \frac{1000}{6} \rfloor - \lfloor \frac{1000}{15} \rfloor - \lfloor \frac{1000}{10} \rfloor + \lfloor \frac{1000}{30} \rfloor = 734$$

Now, get rid of multiples of 7 from here by computing $\lfloor \frac{734}{7} \rfloor = 104$. Hence, there are $630 (= 734 - 104)$ number of multiples of 2, 3, or 5, yet not of 7.

24. The answer is (B). Notice that $Y = \{2, 3, 4, 5, 6, 8, 9, 10, 12, 15, 16, 18, 20\}$. Since, 5, 10, 15, and 20 must be included in the subset of Y, we have 1^4. Now, there should be at least one perfect square in subsets of Y, so there are $7 (= 2^3 - 1)$ possible ways to place at least one perfect squares in subsets of Y. Lastly, there are 6 elements that can be either included or excluded in subset computation, so there are 2^6 ways to place the remaining elements. Hence, there are $1^4 \times (2^3 - 1) \times 2^6 = 448$ ways to choose subsets of Y satisfying the given condition.

25. The answer is (D). Perform casework on the number of 2's in the selection.

- There is no 2. If we let a, b, and c be the number of 3s, 5s, and 7s, then $a + b + c = 5$. Hence, by given condition, $(a, b, c) = (3, 2, 0), (3, 1, 1)$ and $(2, 2, 1)$, i.e, $\frac{5!}{3!2!} + \frac{5!}{3!} + \frac{5!}{2!2!} = 60$ possible ways to choose and arrange five digits other than 2.

- There is one 2. Then, $a + b + c = 4$, so $(a, b, c) = (3, 1, 0), (3, 0, 1), (2, 2, 0), (2, 1, 1), (1, 2, 1)$, i.e., $\frac{4!}{3!} \times 2 + \frac{4!}{2!2!} + \frac{4!}{2!} \times 2 = 38$ ways to choose and arrange four digits other than 2. Since there are 5 spots for 2 to be placed in the beginning, we have $5 \times 38 = 190$ possible ways to choose and arrange five digits.

- There are two 2s. Then, $a + b + c = 3$, so $(a, b, c) = (3, 0, 0), (2, 1, 0), (2, 0, 1), (1, 2, 0), (0, 2, 1), (1, 1, 1)$ so there are 19 ways to choose and arrange three digits other than 2. Since there are $\frac{5!}{2!3!} = 10$ ways to place two 2s in the beginning, we have $19 \times 10 = 190$ possible ways to choose and arrange five digits.

- There are three 2s. Then, $a + b + c = 2$, so $(a, b, c) = (2, 0, 0), (1, 1, 0), (1, 0, 1), (0, 2, 0) (0, 1, 1)$, so there are 8 ways to choose and arrange two digits other than 2. Since there are $\frac{5!}{3!2!} = 10$ ways to place three 2s in the beginning, we have $10 \times 8 = 80$ possible ways to choose and arrange five digits.

In total, there are $410 (= 60 + 190 + 100 + 60)$ ways to make five-digit numbers from the given list.

26. The answer is (D). Without loss of generality, let's assume 2 is selected. Then, there should be other two primes selected from the list with $\frac{9!}{2!7!} = 36$ ways. In other words, 2 appeared 36 times in the summation. Hence, each prime appeared 36 times in the summation, so the sum of all elements in n sets can be written as

$$36 \times (2 + 3 + 5 + 7 + 11 + 13 + 17 + 19 + 23 + 29) = 36 \times 129 = 2^2 \times 3^3 \times 43$$

Since 2 and 3 appear in the given set, 43 must be the other prime not in the list.

27. The answer is (B). From 1 to 9, there are 9 digits. From 10 to 99, there are 180 digits. Now, from 100 to 709, there are 1830 digits. Hence, 2021st digit must be 1, since $2021 = 9 + 180 + 1832$, and we conclude that 1 is the 2021st digit.

28. The answer is (D). Let the number of counterclockwise movement as a and that of clockwise movement as b. Then, $a + b = 7$ and $|a - b| = 3$. Hence, $(a, b) = (5, 2)$ or $(2, 5)$. Therefore, there are $2 \times \binom{7}{2} = 42$.

29. The answer is (B). Have a look at the following figure.

○✓ ○ ✓ ○ ✓ ○ ✓ ○ ✓ ○ ✓ ○

Choosing four seats from the checkmark is enough, so there are $\binom{7}{4} = 35$ possible ways to mark seats for "seat separation."

30. The answer is (D). Arrange four Rs and six Ts, and place five Ss in 11 possible places. Hence, $\binom{10}{6} \times \binom{11}{5} = (42)^2 \cdot 55$. Hence, the largest perfect square that divides the number of arrangements is 42^2.

31. The answer is (E). Let $a = a' + 1$, $b = b' + 6$ and $c = c' + 11$. Then, $c' + 11 \leq 21$ implies that $c' \leq 10$ and $1 \leq a = a' + 1$ implies that $0 \leq a'$. Hence, $0 \leq a' \leq b' \leq c' \leq 10$ implies that there are $\binom{13}{3} = 286$ ways to choose such triplets.

32. The answer is (C). If 2 is used twice, then there are 2□□2, □2□2 and □□22, which can be counted as 9×8, 8×8 and 8×8. If 0 is used twice, then □002 implies that there are 8 possibilities. Likewise, if a number other than 0 or 2 is used twice, then □△□2, □□△2, and △□□2 are formed, which can be counted as 8×8, 8×8 and 8×7. The sum of all possibilities equals 392.

33. The answer is (E). Arranging ten black marbles and three white marbles in a row equals $13!/(10!3!)$. Getting rid of the overcounts for circular permutation, we get 22 arrangements in a circle.

34. The answer is (D). Take a complement. The total number of configurations with seven people is $7!/7 = 720$. On the other hand, if two supervisiors are sitting next to each other, there are $2 \times 5! = 240$ number of configurations. Hence, there are 480 different configurations for seven people to sit around the circle such that two supervisors are seated next to each other.

35. The answer is (E). Switch inequality into equation by adding another variable. Since x, y, and z are natural numbers, we use 1-to-1 correspondence to come up with x', y' and z' such that $x = x' + 1$, $y = y' + 1$ and $z = z' + 1$. Hence, $x' \geq 0$, $y' \geq 0$ and $z' \geq 0$. Therefore, $x' + y' + z' < 17$. This means that $x' + y' + z' = 16, 15, 14, \cdots, 0$. Let w be added to the equation such that $x' + y' + z' + w = 16$. Hence, $\binom{19}{3} = 969$ is the correct answer.

36. The answer is (B). First, there are $\binom{20}{5} = 15504$ number of 6-tuples satisfying $a + b + c + d + e + f = 15$. Since $2^a \cdot 4^b \cdot 3^c \cdot 9^d$ is a multiple of 36, $a + 2b \geq 2$ and $c + 2d \geq 2$. We use complementary counting method to find out that $(a, b, c, d) = (0, 0, 0, 0), (0, 0, 1, 0), (1, 0, 0, 0)$ and $(1, 0, 1, 0)$ should be excluded. Hence, there are 60 bad cases to exclude. The answer is 15444.

37. The answer is (C). Let $\overline{ABCDEF}$ be a six-digit number where 0 is allowed in each spot. According to the condition, $A + B + C + D + E + F = 9$. Using circles and bars, we conclude that there are $\binom{14}{5} = 2002$ number of configurations of $\overline{ABCDEF}$.

38. The answer is (C). First, choose a row for each adult, by $3!$. Then, make sure each adult is seated in one out of four chairs, by 4^3. Then, the rest of the people may be seated in $9 \times 8 \times 7 \times 6 \times 5 \times 4$. Hence, the total number of configurations is $2^{13} \cdot 3^4 \cdot 5 \times 7$. Thus, the sum of bases and exponents equals $2 + 3 + 5 + 7 + 13 + 4 + 1 + 1 = 36$.

39. The answer is (C). Let A be the number of regions colored as yellow, B as green, C as purple and D as blue. Then, $A + B + C + D = 8$ where $A \geq B \geq C \geq D \geq 1$. Hence, $(A, B, C, D) = (5, 1, 1, 1), (4, 2, 1, 1), (3, 3, 1, 1), (3, 2, 2, 1)$, and $(2, 2, 2, 2)$. Since all regions in the figure are "distinct," we consider it equivalent to a rectilinear permutation. Hence,

$$n = \frac{8!}{5!} + \frac{8!}{4!2!} + \frac{8!}{3!3!} + \frac{8!}{3!2!2!} + \frac{8!}{2!2!2!2!}$$
$$= 6496$$

Therefore, there are three distinct digits in n.

40. The answer is (C). First, choose four lockers to be opened by $\binom{10}{4}$. Now, for other six lockers, make sure that wrong keys are assigned to lockers. This is a "derangement." Hence, $\binom{10}{4} \times \left(\frac{6!}{2!} - \frac{6!}{3} + \frac{6!}{4!} - \frac{6!}{5!} + \frac{6!}{6!}\right) = 210 \times 265 = 2 \times 3 \times 5^2 \times 7 \times 53$. Hence, there are five distinct prime factors of n.

41. The answer is (D). Choose a couple that must be selected by $\binom{5}{1}$. Then, choose three couples from remaining four couples by $\binom{4}{3}$. Out of three couples, choose either male or famale from each selected couple by 2^3. Hence, the answer must beh $5 \times 4 \times 8 = 160$.

42. The answer is (B). We must partition $\{1,2,3,4,5,6,7,8\}$ into $\{3,X,Y,Z\}|\{A,B,C,D\}$ where X, Y and Z are greater than 3. Choose $\{X,Y,Z\}$ by $\binom{5}{2}$. Then, partition $\{3,X,Y,Z\}$ into two subsets by three ways, i.e., either $\{3,X\}|\{Y,Z\}$, $\{3,Y\}|\{X,Z\}$ or $\{3,Z\}|\{X,Y\}$. Then, the remaining numbers must go inside $\{A,B,C,D\}$. Partition it into two 2-element subsets by $\binom{4}{2} \times \binom{2}{2}/2$. Hence, we get $30 \times 3 = 90$ different arrangements.

43. The answer is (B). Each term of the expansion of $(1+\sqrt{3}+\sqrt{5})^5$ can be written as $\frac{5!}{a!b!c!}1^a(\sqrt{3})^b(\sqrt{5})^c$. Since p is an integer, we need to make sure that b and c are even. Therefore, $a+b+c = 5$ has six triples, $(5,0,0)$, $(3,2,0)$, $(3,0,2)$, $(1,2,2)$, $(1,4,0)$, and $(1,0,4)$. Hence,

$$p = \frac{5!}{5!}1^5 + \frac{5!}{3!2!}1^3(\sqrt{3})^2 + \frac{5!}{3!2!}1^3(\sqrt{5})^2 + \frac{5!}{2!2!}(\sqrt{3})^2(\sqrt{5})^2 + \frac{5!}{4!}(\sqrt{5})^4 + \frac{5!}{4!}(\sqrt{3})^4$$
$$= 1 + 30 + 50 + 450 + 125 + 45$$
$$= 701$$

44. The answer is (C). Let a, b, c, and d be the face-value of a die that shows up each time we throw it. Then, we must ensure that $1 \leq a \leq b \leq c \leq d \leq 6$. Then, let x_1 be the number of 1's that appeared, x_2 that of 2's, x_3 that of 3's, x_4 that of 4's, $\cdots$, and x_6 that of 6's. Here, $x_1 + x_2 + x_3 + x_4 + x_5 + x_6 = 4$. By circles and bars, we get $\binom{9}{4} = 126$.

45. The answer is (C). If the marbles are placed on top of odd-numbered chairs, then 8 marbles have odd number of chairs between any consecutive pair of chairs. Likewise, if the marbles are placed on top of even-numbered chairs, then 8 marbles have odd number of chairs between consecutive pairs, as well. Hence, the answer must be $2 \times \binom{15}{8}$ or $2 \times \binom{15}{7}$. Since $k \geq 8$, we conclude that $p \times \binom{n}{k} = 2 \times \binom{15}{8}$. Therefore, $p+n+k = 2+15+8 = 25$.

Math Summer Programs

MIT에 언급된, The American Mathematical Society에서 소개하는 여름 수학 캠프는 다음과 같습니다.
- ☑ AwesomeMath
- ☑ Canada/USA Mathcamp
- ☑ Hampshire College Summer Studies in Mathematics (HCSSiM)
- ☑ Texas State Mathworks Honors Summer Math Camp
- ☑ MathILy
- ☑ Program in Mathematics for Young Scientists (PROMYS)
- ☑ The ROSS Program
- ☑ Stanford University Mathematics Camp (SUMaC)
- ☑ Prove It! Math Academy

다음 Q & A는 학부모 및 학생이 자주 하는 질문에 대한 답변입니다.

Q. 위 수학 캠프를 지원할 때, 반드시 AIME Qualifier여야 하나요?
A. 공식적으로 알려진 것은 없지만, AIME Qualifier가 아니더라도, 그에 준하는 성적이 나온 경우, 충분히 경쟁력 있는 Applicant가 될 수 있습니다.

Q. 위 수학 캠프에서 배우는 내용들은 어떠한 내용들이 있나요?
A. 대부분 Number Theory를 기반으로 한 증명 수업을 진행하고, 학생들이 직접 문제를 증명하며 제출하는 방식으로 진행합니다. 다만, 캠프별로 다른 내용들이 진행되므로, 관심 있는 학생들은 위 캠프를 인터넷으로 검색하여, 구체적으로 알아보시기 바랍니다.

Q. Math Summer Camp 혹은 대학 입시에서 공대(혹은 수리계열 관련 학과) 지원 시, AMC 10/12가 좋은 성적이 아닌데, 기입해야 하나요?
A. (제 주관을 말씀드리자면) 경시 시험을 꾸준히 치렀다면, AIME Qualifier가 아니더라도, 성적을 기입하는 것이 맞습니다. 성적 기입을 하지 않는다면, 시험을 보지 않았다고 생각을 하지 않을까 돌이켜 생각해보시면 이해하기가 쉽습니다.
학생 본인이 수학에 관심이 있고, 수학 자체를 즐기는 학생이라면, 시험을 잘 볼 수도 있고 못 볼 수도 있는 것이기 때문에, 자신이 투자한 시간과 에너지에 대한 결과는 Award가 아니더라도, Activity라도 적어야 하지 않을까 하는 생각이 듭니다.

Q. AMC 10/12 (및 AIME) 말고, 다른 경시 시험을 굳이 봐야 하나요?
A. (제 주관을 말씀드리자면) 수학을 좋아하는 학생이, 경시대회 공부를 하는데, AMC 10/12만 치른다는 것도 대학입학사정관의 관점으로 본다면 이상하지 않을까 생각이 듭니다. 미국 내에 Purple Comet Math Meet, ARML, HMMT, PUMaC, SMT, Stanford SMILE, CMIMC, CHMMC, BMT, LMT 등 다양하고 매우 경쟁력 있는 대회들이 있고, 이런 대회를 온라인으로 볼 수 있는 여건이 된다면, 가능하다면 많은 시험을 치러보는 것이 Extracurricular Activity를 가득 채울 수 있는 좋은 기회가 되지 않을까 싶습니다.